London Journal of [illegible]

Issue One: Spring 2016

First published 2016 by the London Journal of Fiction

Cover art by Louis Fratino

ISBN 978-0-9935438-0-7

Designed and typeset
in Bell MT and FreightText Pro

Printed and bound
by Y Lolfa Cyf. in Talybont, Wales

A CIP catalogue reference for this book
is available at the British Library

www.londonjournaloffiction.com

Contents

Submissions to the summer issue are currently open. For more information see our website: www.londonjournaloffiction.com

Preface

In July 2015 the London Journal of Fiction was launched to the world. Our aim was to create a platform for writers which fosters talent and celebrates good writing, regardless of style or genre.

We are extremely grateful to the many hundreds of people who have supported us in this. From the writers who have shared the fruits of their labour, those who have offered their advice and experience, and to the readers who have held everything together with their support and encouragement. All of you have helped to make publishing this issue a possibility.

The publishing industry has changed dramatically in recent years, from the first kindle in 2007 and the launch of submittable in 2009, to the recent growth in new journals, flash and micro fiction. Our journey through the rich landscape of the modern literary community began online and we were overwhelmed at the welcome we received. Kind words and literary offerings began coming in from across London and, soon enough, from much further afield. However it is clear that the demand for print material remains strong. There is a sentimental value associated with the smell of new paper; the physical object on which a piece is printed; the notes scrawled in the margins of a copy borrowed from a friend.

In producing the final contents list for this magazine, with nearly a thousand pieces to choose from, we have been forced to leave out lots of great writing. However we feel the quality of the pieces in these pages reflects the wealth of available talent and the current strength of the literary scene. We hope this continues for many years to come.

Adam Thelwall

Fiction Editorial

Choosing the ten short stories featured in this issue from the towering mountain of talent looming in our submissions inbox was no small feat. There were simply too many good stories, witty writers, and cunning narrators to choose from. The editing table is still hot from all the heat our writers brought to our editorial meetings. And something tells me that, with all this great potential out there, our selection process is not going to get any easier!

Needless to say, it's been an invigorating start for us here at LJF.

Syphoning through a submissions pile is a remarkable way to gauge the collective mood of writers across the globe. Though probably not much has changed since the printing press, I cannot help but point out some tropes which I encountered during my own syphoning-adventure: falling in love in a bar or on the tube, changes of scene inspired by a need to smoke, unemployment, and death. It would be easy to pass these off as 'signs of the times.' But I also wonder if writers grapple with these tropes because of the standpoint from which they view society: their choice to take an introspective step back and observe us all.

On that note!

Within these pages, you will find yourself up against the very real figments of our writers' imaginations: lusty schoolgirls, recovering alcoholics, homophobic parents, brothel madams, and public toilets with answers to all life's questions—just to name a few. Voices, young and old, from all walks of life, will tell you their dreams, fears, failures, and successes. All of them pushed our literary boundaries, taking us on journeys that left us hankering for more good fiction. We hope they do the same for you too.

Arthur Thompson

Poetry Editorial

It is very likely that you might be digesting the Spring 2016 London Journal of Fiction whilst on the toilet. No shame there; in fact this issue of London Journal of Fiction's poetry selection might be particularly suitable. This excellent selection of poetry often tends towards the intimate, and it might be during such private moments that London Journal of Fiction should be read. A genre which so often is very personal becomes immediately accessible to the reader when it concerns constipation, as Thomas Pescatore's 'Geschlossen' does. 'Birthday' includes a radio hosts scornful comments on a woman who steals toilet paper at a riot; in his classism it seems he has forgotten his own bodily functions.

Many of the poems presented here borrow from the narrative. Big stories are told with few words, and we hope that dispersed within the longer narratives, these images might grow. The bathos in 'Man Drowns in Cruise Ship Pool' is both magnificent and mundane when read alongside Jack Granath's ridiculous whale-bear, but after Jeremy Clarke's 'Flying to Eritrea', the whale-bear becomes something more terrible. In this issue, the prominence of narrative structure to our poetry selection might just take steps to open up and avoid unnecessary navel-gazing.

We can of course not guess when our readers will open their copy of London Journal of Fiction, but we hope that when you do, these poems will speak not only for themselves but also to you. Be it on the toilet, in the back-seat of a car, or a cruise-ship pool.

Marjam Idriss

With special thanks to the following people,
whose support and generosity has been vital in getting this magazine all the way through to print:

Cynthia Lee Smet

Rahim Velji

Øyunn Lohne Idriss

Slightly Fizzy, White

Julia Coleman

"My name is Della Healey and I am an alcoholic..."

On her wedding day she appeared on the landing looking dutifully radiant or so she thought. Her father said she looked natty; not intending to wound, but natty was not beautiful and natty was nowhere to be found in Brides magazine.

She let the word pass through her; scuttle over her grave, before she shelved it neatly away in the carefully catalogued library of words and phrases that had long bitten into her - the child who might put her fingers in the lion's cage.

Such words and phrases had littered her youth like the bloody remains of rabbits left flattened at the side of the road, but her husband had looked at her the way he ought and the day went ahead as planned.

Her mother's own family had taken pleasure in frequently telling the younger members that they should not have so much of it and she herself should, as a consequence, never go thinking she was anything special. In turn, her mother sent such portents like final reminders; bills that shot through the letterbox, slapping onto the doormat, in red print, intended to bring anyone who got any outlandish ideas about being happy or free firmly back into line. It was a family where no one knew wonderful and that was how they liked it.

Now she wonders if it's the lot of the guilty; that desire to be punished for failing to stay in line, although in keeping with family tradition (she sighs when she thinks about it) she had never shone at anything.

Then, just like that the benefits people decided that despite her status as a recovering alcoholic, she ought to contribute; get her backside out of the orange plastic 'sharing' chair and there she was - a cleaning operative (get her!) in Accident and Emergency. Only this time she was not covered in her own blood and vomit from a fall off a bar stool in 'The Dog' on the Archway Road after an enjoyable afternoon on the Beaujolais - immediately followed by a heady evening of cocktails.

She'd met Sheila in the 'Ladies' at lunchtime, and they'd locked themselves into the end cubicle and glugged whisky from a bottle she'd smuggled in her handbag, to complement the Beaujolais. Beaujolais; whisky? She must have been drunk! There they were, giggling and gulping down the sweet fire; Della perched on the cistern, and, on the loo seat, trying to light a cigarette; her new and second best friend Sheila - second best as in well behind a bottle of slightly fizzy white. It was Sheila who insisted the publican call an ambulance and who after helping her into it and sweetly tucking the blanket around her, she never saw again. Ditto the whisky and the handbag.

Her slide off a thousand bar stools had begun on Millennium Eve. The party at the local golf club saw everyone in fancy dress, and she had looked forward to it in a way she hadn't looked forward to anything else in a while, though she had no idea why. She had 'a nice husband, a good job in further education, just about everything; you're a lucky girl' they all agreed, but the tone in their voices had more than a hint of consolation prize.

The Millennium party had been disappointing. She felt fat in the Betty Boop costume, and then her friend Louise announced she was expecting twins. Not one, but two surprises brought by the stork. Della had tried to feel the love but despite the endless humping with her own very pleasant husband at all the correctly measured times on all the correctly counted days, Della had yet to get a visit.

The doctor said 'Count your blessings' but agreed to tests that would prove inconclusive and then everybody said 'Wait, it'll happen, you'll see, Mother Nature won't be rushed' but at home on the sofa watching television night after night there was an unnatural silence between them.

The placating tailed off eventually, and in the end it was just her mother who came upon her in the street smelling of Lambrusco (Della not her mother) and weeping openly (her mother not Della).

This caused passers-by to stop and give Della terrible looks, and to ask her mother if she was all right and was Della troubling her? Oh boy was that the wrong thing to ask her mother! Was Della troubling her? Oy vey! It didn't matter that they weren't Jewish, or that Della was trying to vomit into her coat pocket and pass it off as a tickly throat, nor even that her mother was busy engaging complete strangers in a conversation about Della's imminent demise under the spell of the evil Dr Lambrini, to the point where some of them joined in to scold Della or worse; to share in her mother's pleading.

She spent the year losing. She lost weight, and then she lost some more weight. She lost a couple of friends who just couldn't face her, and then she lost a couple whose husbands were worried she might take them down with her.

Then in late November, she lost her best friend Carrie's daughter Rosie in a very large branch of Boots the Chemist. It wasn't quite the disaster it could have been; she was found quite quickly; still strapped into her buggy; fast asleep and none the wiser. It took them a little longer to discover where Della was -not that she had gone far, just to the pub across the road to enjoy a Spritzer – without the soda water. She never saw Carrie again.

It took her quite a bit longer to lose her job. She can't remember too much about it, except that Bob Sugar from the Union sat by her side talking ten to the dozen in her defence, but by that time she had pretty much burned every boat in the harbour. Hitting the Principal's Toyota on entering the car park one Tuesday morning hadn't helped much, but hitting it as she exited on the Tuesday night she sensed had pretty much sealed the deal.

Some weeks later she resigned but on her way out of the building she tripped, not once but twice. On the first occasion she saved herself, wobbled and walked on. On the second occasion, some two minutes later; she flew; landed face down and then slid across the newly polished herringbone patterned woodblock floor, like Bambi on that frozen pond. Her arms and legs splayed; skirt around her thighs; she overtook a rather surprised group of Media in Practice students on their way to lunch, one of whom called out cheerfully "Congratulations Miss, you made the Curling team!"

Bob Sugar picked her up before escorting her, hobbling, to her car and spending a few moments consoling her before fitting her seatbelt and slamming the door. That slam was the most terrible slam she ever heard. That slam heralded the last of her weekly, hollow vows to sober up and was the beginning of all attempts to get just as drunk and disorderly as she possibly could.

She would show them, she would give them all a ringside seat to her one woman show 'Despair and Desperation' starring, featuring and all about Della. She impressed upon all who met her the actions that belied the words 'My name is Della Hardcastle and I am an alcoholic' without ever saying them, until their own despair and desperation made them fold themselves into suitcases and send themselves packing rather than have to endure another moment. She waved them off cheerfully indifferent, or muttered into her fizz about their betrayals, and fell off bar stools or over pavement kerbs and as she was helped up or into the ambulance she told the kindly of *their* lack of staying power, of *their* betrayals.

Finally, she lost her husband, but before he went they had to discuss The Problem one last time. Given that she *was* the problem, there was little she could say. Alan spent quite some time saying 'This is just not you Della. I keep wondering just who is this creature'. She was so drunk that she kept looking around for a Parakeet or a Terrapin, or Godzilla beside her on the sofa. Giggling, she asked him to describe the creature using his favourite rude words and he sighed, picked up his bag, crossed the room and shut the door quietly behind him. Puzzled, she poured the rest of the bottle into her glass and put on the television, Countdown was on and some wag had tried the word 'Temperance'.

About two further years into her inebriant stride, and following innumerable large white wines in 'The Hay Wain" on the Chalk Farm Road, she made a two a.m. phone call to a recently 'ex' boyfriend telling him she'd swallowed a packet of pills. This was SUICIDE ATTEMPT NUMBER ONE. In truth she'd lied, but he dutifully rushed to her side, even asked her to marry him.

SUICIDE ATTEMPT NUMBER TWO? Imagine Parliament Hill just as the sun is setting on a glorious day. Just as the very young are being settled into fresh bedding after warm baths, and the rest of us are settling down to watch Holby City. Now think skinny, grubby woman at the till in Tesco Metro, with a bottle of fizzy white in one hand, and not quite enough money in the other.

She was short by twenty-six pence.

The assistant; 'Amanda, How Can I Help?' and then the Manager; 'Ms Helen Price, How Can I Help?' wouldn't budge. Della wasn't finding either of them terribly helpful.

The long queue waited in an irritable silence. She pleaded sweetly, harangued to no avail before she called the Manager a 'minging bitch.' Della said *she* should have a little self-respect and followed that cracking line with 'I will be contacting your Head Orifice' before she picked up a dangerous looking packet of Extra Strong Mints and pointed it in a threatening manner at the queue.

An elderly woman, about three people away stepped forward; put her hand on Della's arm and said quietly, 'Hello Della, you won't remember me but I used to live next door to you when you were just a little girl. I know your mother.'

If called upon to remember the episode, she remembers looking down at the old lady's claw-like hand that now rested on her arm, and, it's painful but she can still remember the musical hum the bottle made as it slid from her own clammy hand and hit the floor. She can even remember the splash of cold liquid on her legs, and the old lady's gasp at the shock of it and how she said quietly "Oh, my new stockings."

Della leaned in close towards the Manager's face and sneered "Get the mop then Linda" before she flung the door open and tottered up the Highgate Road having flung the coins to the floor where they rolled around in the smashed glass before teetering to a halt in the sticky wine.

As she passed the posh boys school next to the tennis courts she came across Ronnie lying on the grass at the entrance to the park. He woke up as she was going through his pockets but when she accused him of touching her up, he apologised profusely and then bought her a number of large white wines in 'The Flask' until closing time.

They got on like a house on fire after that, getting a 'take-away' bottle of fizzy white and walking arm in arm up Swain's Lane, shouting the lyrics to Elton John's 'I'm Still Standing' even though Ronnie fell over a low wall and then a bollard on the zebra crossing. If pushed, Della will remember what a sweat it was getting him hard round the back of some exclusive children's boutique on Highgate Hill by way of a thank you, and what a pleasant trip down memory lane it makes for.

She woke up in The Whittington Hospital at about four 'o' clock several afternoons later, with a very sore throat from having her stomach pumped on account of the paracetamol. There was no reason for it, merely a lack of reason, I suppose.

Her sister Claire was at her bedside, all the way from Canada. She took Della home and cleaned up the house. When she felt better they took all the empties to the recycling centre in a shiny black Megane. As they smashed the bottles, Della asked when the hire agreement ended. Claire said, "Lewis wants me back in Toronto by Monday evening our time. He has a conference in Buffalo and someone needs to walk the dog." Della said "You're as happy as me then" and Claire roared on the gas by way of reply. After a long silence she said "Nearly a hundred fucking bottles Della?" to which she replied (in the little girl voice that had always won her father from her mother) "The Co-op was doing a Buy One Get One Free." They laughed all the way home and all the way through Chicken Dupiaza and Aloo Saag. Della barely touched hers of course, but some went down, and even stayed down for a while.

They sat through a more miserable dinner at their mother's house on the Sunday. She said all the usual empty stuff. 'No person should want to end their own life, that is a business for God only' or, 'what did I do so wrong, tell me?' until they could stand it no longer. Then she said, 'If your Father had lived to see this.' Della looked at her sister, did a comical double-take, and said, "My F.. Father is... dead?" Claire snorted into her trifle and their mother looked at Della for a long time with her puzzled, rheumy eyes, before she pushed her plate away, stood up and said, 'That's fresh fruit in that jelly that is; other people's mothers use tinned.' Then she turned her hunched, hostile, back and left the room.

They slept together that night in Della's bed, curled up like they had as children and as Claire said goodbye to her at the airport the next day she said, 'All that chucking up is ruining your lovely teeth'. Then she kissed her on the forehead, picked up her bag and almost ran through the gates with it.

It took Della almost seventy-two hours to get completely hammered, and then swallow the thirteen paracetamol that made it SUICIDE ATTEMPT NUMBER THREE but Claire did not get a return flight. Some things are unforgivable, and on the few occasions they have seen one another since, even though they smile and hug, Della knows when she looks into her sister's eyes, that trying to kill herself so soon after Claire's departure is one of them.

The Doctor who came to talk with her when she woke said she was just one of the lucky ones, that her organs had somehow survived the onslaught, that other people have died from much less, some of them terribly slowly; in agony. That's the thing with paracetamol, it's tricky; it's a roll of the dice. I guess Della just threw a lucky number, though nowadays if she has a headache she uses that well-known cure, the bang it off the wall approach; rather than risk her liver.

The next time she woke there were two other people beside the bed. One was Colin Cleary, who ran a local Charity for Drug and Alcohol Mis-Users, and the other was Colin Cleary – though her vision did return to normal after a few days.

In a quiet, matter of fact way, Colin explained to Della that the bank had finally repossessed the house. This seemed fair enough, given that she hadn't paid the mortgage in a very long time.

He also explained that they had allowed the bailiffs in to take the contents; in lieu of other debts. This had been authorised by Alan who wanted a little closure to go with his Decree Absolute and whose name was still on the mortgage deeds, and whose pleas to her to 'sort it out' had gone unheeded in among the white grape fumes.

She listened, nodded; tucked tight into the stiff hospital sheets she felt small, safe. Colin Cleary was very calm, very gentle on her. He didn't shout, wring his hands or shake his head and ask 'Why, why?' over and over. This was all right. This was okay. This she could cope with.

There was more, he said. It got worse, he said. She looked at him puzzled. She had lost her job, her home, her husband, her friends and everything she owned and there was worse?

Colin Cleary looked at Della with a terrifying kindness before he said, "In the garden of your house, the bailiffs found a rabbit hutch with the remains of a small animal inside. There was no food in the hutch, and the water bottle lay on the ground nearby, hidden in the long grass."

Of course she wishes with all her despicable heart that no animals had been harmed in the making of this alcoholic but despite her desperate avoidance tactics; the absolute agony, was, at that moment, met, squared up to and looked in the eye and later despite her furious attempts to stare it down, it would be quietly, unconditionally accepted.

But at that moment she just lay there stunned and then after a while she found that reedy, thin little-girl voice again and told Colin Cleary that the animal had been a rescue rabbit she'd adopted on a whim from someone she met in 'The Washington' a pub on England's Lane; because she was lonely and had no babies to love. She had called the rabbit Jessica, after the movie, and it was what she would have called a daughter had she managed one.

He continued to look at her with a kindly understanding she would never understand, and for a long time he smiled an encouraging, gentle smile; willing her to find the way but she could not, would not, was not ready to abandon that little girl and her little girl voice and her little girl hurts and her very, very, tiny girl need to run from the truth and have her daddy take away the reality as he had always done.

Colin Cleary was not her father, though he may have loved her just as deeply at that moment, for he sat by her and waited in the silence just like that little rabbit had waited, starving slowly while Della sat on the sofa and cried into her fizzy white because she had no babies.

A while later he cleared his throat and said he said he was very sorry about her not being able to have any babies, but he was a lot sorrier about that rabbit. Then he took her hand as she cried, sobbed, and finally wailed.

From deep within her sorry soul, hot salty tears welled up in her jaundiced eyes and ran down her cheeks til they dripped off the end of her nose. Every rasping sob sounded like a death rattle, which is, I guess, exactly what they were, for she had finally stopped drinking. It was September 27th 2011, and she suddenly had a perspective other than the one she'd had for years – the boring, the deeply unattractive and totally addictive drug they never warn you about in school – self-pity.

Colin Cleary turned out to be her saviour, though he was a man without faith. He achieved nothing through prayer; only through words; fired off directly at her or slipped sideways into a conversation; going unnoticed until she lay in bed, sleepless the following night. An ex-addict himself, he entered into no games with her other than the one called survival. He made her no promises, and gave her no reassurances other than the fact that she hadn't drunk alcohol since that day and so far today.

Slowly, steadily, flinching at every turn; she crawled from the mire that her life had become. The sticking plasters that had always come unstuck were carefully replaced with zips that Colin helped her to zipper; the teeth in organised rows; over sewn with solid stitches; good quality thread.

She chose not to drink each day on waking and several hundred times a day after that. She still chooses; if not with such frequency but with only the most tenuous of footholds on the world and nothing more spectacular than sobriety as the prize. No riches or fame or pot of gold at the end of the rainbow, actually no rainbows, just endless driving rain.

Today, she is Della Healey, non-drinking alcoholic and now cleaning operative; oh and tenant of one small flat, long-leased to her by a housing association known for its work with recovering addicts and ex-offenders and let's face it she was pretty offensive.

Also, and really the whole reason I began telling you this story, loving and beloved partner of Bassel. He's an anaesthetist at the hospital. He fled Syria when they were murdering their people in a less overt, more particular fashion; his family among them. He told her the story of his long journey the first night they slept together. He said when he had looked into her eyes he had recognised a kindred spirit, a soul who had wandered close to the edge stared down into the black and somehow found the way back.

Oh and there's one more thing, she came on shift this morning at 6am and as she was mopping up the blood left on the floor after a stabbing victim went into theatre, she fainted. Sometimes, even when you are used to it, a lot of blood in one go can have that effect; especially before breakfast.

They took her blood pressure, all the usuals but they couldn't find a problem. She would have gone on her way there and then but Aoife a little student nurse wouldn't hear of it. Aoife's the eldest of maybe hundreds of children by the sound of it, and bossy doesn't do her justice.

So there's Della laid on the gurney and Bass has been bleeped down from theatre and is now looking worried beside her as Tom, one of the junior doctors feels her belly and says "Mmm, could you be pregnant, Della?" She looks at Bass; he's heard *her* story too and she swallows with a painful brick-filled throat and says aloud that she wasn't able to have children; sadly.

Aoife flushes an agonised red at the thought of such calamity and Della tries to give her a reassuring smile. Meanwhile Tom rubs cold jelly onto her belly, fiddles around, and then runs the ultrasound over her cool, quivering skin as he studies the screen.

Bass searches urgently and meets Della's eyes; knows she cannot bear to look at that screen but Aoife breaks the silence with a little cry, stifled by a quick hand over her own mouth which makes Della tear her eyes away from Bass and look up at that screen..

And there you were, in glorious monochrome, all twenty-two wondrous weeks of you; curled up; thumb in mouth; heart going ten to the dozen.

And here I am; snivelling Uriah Heep humble, grateful with all my guilty, galloping heart. "My name is Della Healey, and I am going to be a mother..."

The Road Beneath the Street

Nikki Carr

Tons of hot metal
catapulting over gravel skin
withered and cracked by weight weary from
answering constant visitors knocks
at her door, which caused
bumps to form like kosher dills
plucked from freshly salted brine
naturally ripe for fermentation,
yet sewn together
with tar and cement
like a patchwork quilt
only to leave cracks
and wrinkles down sides
of her face.

Alp Horn

Jason Makansi

When the staffer at the Swiss Embassy in DC called Darby Timken, she feigned nonchalance.

"Yes, of course I still play the Alp horn."

She had learned to play the instrument as an exchange student in Switzerland the summer she turned sixteen. The low, soothing tones permeating the mountainside rushed back to her.

"And when is the gig?" she asked, rustling some papers, pretending to look for a calendar.

How did they find me, she wondered, before a vague recollection surfaced of filling out an on-line form at musicians.net.

"The Embassy's annual garden party will take place on the first Friday in November," said the man, each word stiffly accentuated, mannerisms Darby associated with the Swiss.

The Swiss family she had lived with was anything but soothing but wooden certainly would suffice. If you so much as tripped on a raised cobblestone walking along their crooked, narrow streets, they'd look at you like you broke the law. Only the Swiss would hold a garden party in November, Darby thought.

"We're absolutely delighted. Alp horn players are so rare in America. Will you arrive with your own instrument or shall we provide one?"

Darby desperately needed the money. Playing first chair French horn in a third tier orchestra didn't pay much and that was as far as Darby had advanced in her career.

"I'd just as soon use yours. I'll warm up before the gig. You will cover all the travel expenses?"

"Yes, well, of course, Ms. Timken. The musical portion of the event will begin at 2:00 pm sharp. If you would, kindly let me know when in advance of the concert you would prefer to pick up the horn. In the meantime, I shall send you the music we wish to hear and an advance to cover your initial expenses."

Darby realized she would have to find somewhere to practice. On her way from BWI airport to the Embassy to pick up the instrument, she instructed the cabbie to divert off the Baltimore-Washington Parkway and take New York Avenue. She grew up in DC and remembered some dated and hopefully still inexpensive motels along that route. Surely one would be cheap, largely empty, and she could pocket the balance of the Embassy's generous per diem. At some point, she'd have to decide whether to visit her father. Darby had not spoken to him since high school.

She spotted the Court Walk Motel, "vacancy" lit up, a narrow parking lot between the rooms and the sidewalk. Seems good enough, she thought, as the taxi waited at a traffic light. The neighbourhood had seen better days, but the motel itself didn't appear any worse than some of the apartment complexes in her Huntsville, Alabama neighbourhood. The important thing was only a few cars were present.

Darby hopped out when the driver pulled up alongside the curb at the Embassy. She exited the driver's side. She paused and then took the clasps out of her gold-flecked hair and the threaded mass fell to her derrière. It pulled at her scalp like English ivy in a hanging planter. Even at age fifty, she knew it was a difficult asset to ignore, probably her only one. She heard the driver gasp, then saw him smile, revealing one gold cap among a set of chaotically placed teeth.

"Just wait here. Keep the meter running," she instructed. The air was crisp, wafting to cold.

"Lady, you the boss."

She returned a few minutes later, deliberate in her step, cradling the lengthy awkward instrument.

"Damn, don't just sit there. Help me with this thing!"

The driver didn't move and kept his window rolled up. He reached for the steering wheel like he was going to leave.

She rapped on the glass, and yelled, "It's luggage, okay?"

Finally, he got out.

"Too big, too much." he said. Then he gestured with both of his arms. "Too long."

The scratchy rumble of his voice seemed to aim at a place much higher than he was tall.

She looked back nervously at the embassy's entrance. "No, it isn't. We can tie it to the roof or something. It's only a few blocks away, where I'm going," she lied.

"No rope, boss lady. No tie up. Illegal, too."

"Wait. I got a better idea. We'll just let it hang out the window."

"No. Illegal. I lose license."

"And drive very carefully...."

She thumbed a twenty out of a roll of bills, courtesy of the Embassy advance, in her bra.

"That's on top of the fare and tip."

At the Court Walk, she got the taxi driver's card. At least he would be familiar with the ordeal when she had to return. She asked for the least expensive room available. The proprietor, an Asian woman with teeth worse than those of the cab driver, said sixty dollars cash.

Darby had brought an overnight bag with some toiletries and the outfit she would need for the concert. She noticed a group of younger men congregated on the second floor landing. She leaned the shapely horn against the outside wall next to the office door.

She breathed deeply, acknowledging her memory had failed her. When she learned to play the alp horn, it had been sitting on the porch of a Swiss home halfway up a mountain, owned by friends of her host family. She remembered it being long but not twice as long as she was tall. What was she thinking? Hopefully her lung power wouldn't fail her too.

"Would you help me carry this to my room?" she asked. The woman's face didn't even twitch. Darby peeled a ten dollar bill off her roll. The woman slowly got up, scratched at her hair, rubbed at her bottom, turned away for what seemed like a minute to do something else, turned back towards Darby, and then passed through the metal door from the "office" to the tiny corridor space, separated by a bullet proof shield.

"What do with this?" the woman asked, pointing at the horn.

"I play it."

"You play with it? You play with it, with who? How you play a with this, kinky girl?"

"No, I mean play it, blow into it. It's a horn, a musical instrument."

"Ah, okay, whatever you say," she said with a mischievous smile. She picked up one end.

On the second floor landing down from her room, the men were looking out at the cars rushing by on the street. Darby proceeded and inserted the key. Then she glanced once again at the men. Their commotion suggested to her she had definitely been noticed. She couldn't hear what they were saying, but one of them pointed, another smiled.

Immediately on opening the door, she realized the horn would barely fit into the room. She rushed out the door, and yelled at the woman.

"Ma'am, do you have any larger rooms?"

"Nice large rooms for hourly customers," she yelled back over her shoulder.

She could hear the men laughing. Darby closed the door, sat on her bed, and started sobbing, fists pressed into her tightly closed eyes, the anguish of those years flooding back at her. Her elderly father, now according to her sister, suffering from the later stages of Alzheimer's, didn't live but a few miles away in the posh Northwest section of the city she grew up in. She didn't care what this motel looked like, smelled like, or what those men outside were thinking, anything was better than staying with him.

She had seen her father at her mother's funeral ten years ago. Darby spoke to him through her sister. She'd manage to eke out a living playing in the Huntsville Symphony Orchestra for several decades, supplemented by contract work with orchestras in nearby Atlanta, Nashville, and Chattanooga. She didn't need anyone's help, certainly not his.

She felt empty after the tears. She considered herself in the mirror visible from the small bed. Then she grew determined. Time to quit belly-aching, as her mother would say. She bounced once then jumped from the bed, the dust hanging in the air before it settled back down on the thin brown blanket fit for a barracks.

She remembered what captivated and enraged her about this instrument. Unlike her French horn, you couldn't be intimate with an alp horn. The tubes of her French horn were an extension of her lung cavity and windpipe, the source of air, the instrument's source of life. The tactile connection between fingers and levers was unmistakable.

The Alp horn's bell was removed, like a tin can at the end of a string. But, the sound, deep, penetrating, and soft, was meant for ears miles away. At sixteen, she felt connected to the entire world. The horn's lament penetrated every hollow and cave, every small enclave of homes. For weeks, she spent as much time with the instrument as she could. It helped keep her sane amongst her host family until their son, two years older than Darby, returned from a lengthy sojourn. He couldn't have been more different from his parents, warm, expressive sensitive. They had a romance that lasted two weeks before she returned home. They exchanged one set of letters.

The first note reverberated in the room like an avalanche of logs rumbling through a cave. Her ears smarted. She paused to regain her balance. She couldn't play the thing inside, obviously. Now what? Then she heard a distinct yell, barely muffled though porous, crumbling cinderblock.

"For the love of God! What now?"

The knock on her door came seconds later. Darby first parted the curtains of the window, revealing a woman nearly a foot taller than her, blouse buttoned crookedly, hair dishevelled, arms wrapped around her thin body, pushing her cleavage up to her sallow cheeks. Darby opened the door.

"Wot the hell?" the bewildered woman asked.

"Sorry, I know. It almost blew me into the next room."

"Really? Then you would've landed on top of me and that John in there, screaming about coitus interruptus and payment interruptus..."

"I'm really sorry, but I must practice for a gig on Friday."

"What's today?"

"Wednesday?"

"Okay, Miss Horn Toad," she said, jutting her right hip out, and leaning that direction, "of all the places you could have picked to play whatever it was made that john's brains in there plug up his hole down there..."

"I had to stay somewhere cheap. Musicians don't make much money."

"Neither do whores. What is that thing, anyway?"

Darby opened the door wider to give her a look.

"Well, I'll be a skinny bitch in a ditch. You mind if I borrow that thing? That John next door sees me riding it, maybe he'd only d'mand half his money back."

Darby thought she had heard every sexual innuendo associated with every orchestral instrument in her lifetime.

"I would if it was mine," Darby said, her voice lilting upward, "but it belongs to the Swiss Embassy."

"You shittin' me?"

"No! That's the gig I'm practicing for, the Embassy's annual garden party."

The prostitute shifted her weight, jutting out the opposite hip, her look of disbelief dissipating.

"Okay, I be making a deal wit' you. You practice all you want. When you through, you let me burrow it a few hours. Okay? I could make some serious money. What's yo' name, honey?"

"Darby. And yours?"

"Portia. Remember, we got a deal, okay?"

Darby agreed. She had little choice. She closed the door and turned her attention to the room and the horn. The only way she was going to practice this thing was if the bell hung outside the door and she stood by the bathroom at the far end of the room.

She laid the sheet music on the bed and started pushing air through the instrument to warm it up. Alp horn music isn't complicated. Getting the sound right was more about exercising her lungs and lips than musical technique.

Darby remembered how she fell in love with the sound of a French horn. Her father took her to hear the National Symphony Orchestra at the Kennedy Center, a daddy-daughter evening that featured Brahms First Symphony. The lilting entrance of the melody in the third movement was carried by the strings, then the long motif topped off by the horns. Soon after, Darby asked to take lessons.

Strange, she thought, how a few notes could chart the direction of your entire life, not unlike the wrong few minutes with a boy.

Her motel room was getting cold even with the door just cracked open.

She had barely gotten through the first line of her sheet music when she heard more commotion outside her door, then saw movement through the crack between the two halves of the window shades. The young men had moved to just outside her door.

What the hell, she thought. They reminded her of the men who gathered at the corner convenience store in the Huntsville neighbourhood she'd lived in for years. Normally, she didn't fear these people, but normally there weren't five of them breathing on her front door. She couldn't let anything happen to the instrument. She thought about calling the woman at the front desk but then remembered her apathy. She thought about calling the police. Then she calmed down.

"Yes?" Darby asked, protected by her door.

"We just wondered what this sound is. You're causing accidents out there, almost." The man wearing a cute brown derby with a small red feather on its side did the talking.

"Well, I made some bad calculations," she said.

She added, "The instrument is too long to fit in my room. But I have to practice for a gig on Friday."

"I know that problem. I got a instrument that don't fit either." He nonchalantly brought his right hand to his crotch and lifted his equipment, then smiled, revealing very well-kept teeth.

Darby was relieved when his cohorts chuckled and shushed him off.

"Hey, you talking to a lady," said the one with the hat.

"Gentlemen, I really have to get serious. Would you mind?" She paused. They didn't look like they were going to budge.

"Nice hat, by the way," she added, "what's your name?"

"Rafael." He grinned. He has a nice smile and a pleasant baby face, Darby thought.

"Where this 'insterment' come from? I never seen one." Rafael asked.

"Switzerland. They blow this thing in the mountains. I'm performing at the Swiss Embassy."

"Fer real?"

Darby looked towards the street.

"You should have seen me trying to haul it in a taxi."

"Lady, we seen you when you drive up." He pointed to the end of the balcony.

"I like ta be performing at a embassy..." another one mumbled.

"Isn't every day a lady brings a instrument worthy of a embassy to a shithole like this," Rafael said.

Darby smiled. "Not just any embassy, the Swiss embassy. They're the toughest people in Europe. They're surrounded by mountains. Hard to invade and then it's harder to get out."

"We'll let you alone then, lady. C'mon guys..." Rafael said, drifting down the landing.

She turned around, and started to close the door as much as she could, but not before one of the men commented on her hair.

"Lady, brushing your hair would be, like, a job!"

"I'll take that as a compliment!"

"And well you should!"

Darby went back in and looked over the next few lines of the music. She ate the chips and crackers and drank from the bottle of water she kept from the flight.

Her thoughts drifted back to that summer. She remembered the Swiss being devoid of emotion. She could imagine all of these people in the mountains, heeding the call of the horn, robotically gathering at some central point. If the call was to sing, they'd sing. If the call were to go slaughter people in the next country, well, they'd probably invade. After she returned home and her pregnancy was discovered, she informed the boy and the letters ended. She burned the one she had.

She tried to bury the sound of the alp horn with the memories. She couldn't recall why she had listed it when she saw it as an option the on-line form.

Darby was just finding a groove when there was another knock at the door. She looked up. The afternoon sunlight revealed smudges and streaks in the window glass. The proprietor lady was peering in impatiently.

"How long this go on?" she asked when Darby opened the door.

"It's going to be a while."

The proprietor gestured to the crowd on the sidewalk. Darby was astonished to see the people milling about, gazing towards her room.

"This no good. Bring police. No need police here!"

This is crazy, Darby thought, playing an instrument that begged for the air of an open mountaintop in a cinder block cell in the ghetto. Yet, a crowd had formed. She had an idea. She motioned to the men at the end of the landing. They ambled over.

"I'll take this horn to the parking lot." she said. "I've got to practice! I need your help. You guys can collect money from the crowd while I play. I don't want any of it. Just occupy the crowd."

She explained to the men that the notes from the Alp horn are considered "from God" because they can't be made with keys or holes along the length of the pipe.

"Tell them it's the sound of the gospel from a faraway land," she suggested.

Rafael said, "I like the sound of that, God and money always be goin' together!"

As she played, rotund ladies in colourful clothing, children at their side, a few who looked homeless, tried to get up close. Darby told the men from the balcony that it was okay for kids to approach but no one else. She didn't want anyone to damage the instrument but children who wanted to touch it were okay. At one point, she counted maybe thirty people gathered, awed, perplexed, or just curious. Even the proprietor came out to have a listen.

The guys rapped on windows and car hoods and encouraged drivers to stop and roll their windows down for a sound sensation they'd never hear again. Some of them did, causing a traffic tie up in a part of the city where drivers normally wouldn't stop for a body bleeding in the middle of the street. Horns blared. As she took deep breaths in between notes, she could hear automobile sound systems blasting everything from Gangsta rap to Mariachi. But the alp horn prevailed while gridlock ensued. She thought she saw one woman praying. She didn't know if everyone was paying for her performance or if they were scared of the guys, but Rafael's roll of bills kept growing.

In Switzerland, they used to say the Alp horn mesmerizes the countryside with its natural harmonics. It works in the city, too, Darby learned.

The Embassy gig was little different than other outdoor concerts Darby had performed for decades, except she was the guest performer of honour. The audience listened politely and applauded. After the simple rendition of the melody from the Swiss National Anthem, they applauded a little louder.

Afterwards, Darby asked the attaché if she could return the horn the next day. She explained where she had learned to play and the sentimental value it held for her to play it again so many years later. She'd probably blow all the money she saved staying in a low-rent motel on taxis back and forth. But what the hell? She was in the throes of the after-performance euphoria.

On the ride home, she even blew a few notes from the taxi, the bell of the horn hanging from the window on the passenger side. She laughed and told her driver he didn't need to honk.

She brought the horn back to the Court Walk and dropped it off with Portia. It fit in her room. Then Darby had several hours to kill. She sat on her bed and pondered and finally decided it was now or never. Her sister had pleaded with her to visit him for years. She wasn't normally superstitious but there was good fortune in those low tones. The street performance proved that.

How long could you bury an episode so hurtful, a memory so awkward, so obstructive, it refused to remain where you always left it to die? She decided she would not remind her father how he had forced her to bring the baby to term and put it up for adoption. The past would be the past. She would only try to find out if he remembered when they had first heard the Brahms Symphony together. And then sit politely with him while he talked, if that's what he wanted to do. And, to her surprise, he did remember and she would never forget that.

Portia woke her up the next morning, rapping on the door.

"This is a stick with a kick when you're turning a trick! I made twenty extra dollars last night."

"I guess I shouldn't ask?" Darby raised her hand, shielding her eyes against the sunlight.

"Ah, come on now, Darby girl. I just pretended with it. Besides, damn thing's made of wood. I could get splinters..." Portia smiled.

Later in the morning, Darby saw Rafael at the end of the landing, smoking a cigarette, rocking back and forth on the balls of his feet. He noticed her and tipped his derby.

"Yo, when you doin' yer practicin' agin? We cleared close to a C spot yesterday!"

"That's great, but would you be kind enough to use a buck or two to get me a cup of coffee?"

He strutted off immediately down the clanging metal stairs as if nothing was more important at that moment. She looked out at the street scene, so normal compared to two days ago.

He returned with a large Styrofoam cup with a flimsy lid, and handed it to her while looking at his feet.

"Thank you," she said.

Then he looked into her face, with a shy grin. "Here, you take fifty dolla."

"But..."

"Absolutely. You was the performer. We was just your agent, or manager, or somethin'."

Darby stared hard at Rafael. "I don't need the money," she said firmly.

"Lady, anyone look like you stayin' in a shithole like this with a insterment like that, need the money."

She relented and accepted the bills. She stood enjoying the bright sunshine while Rafael walked the landing and down the stairs.

"You know, you could hear that damn thing ten blocks away!" he yelled from the sidewalk. "Even during rush hour!" he added, and waved.

Pensioner's Concession

Mark Brandi

1. Five days ago.

We stand there, looking at the blue waterproof mattress cover, not knowing what to say. The bed is empty, a thin blanket crumpled on the floor. Soiled, white sheets.

A nurse enters, hesitates. Looks at you. She must notice the resemblance. The crooked Roman nose.

'Are you alright?' she says.

You choke out some words, your voice suddenly strange to my ears. 'We were visiting my dad, he ...'

Her eyes go wide. First at you, then at me. She chews her lip like a teenager. 'Is that... Tom?'

I see your cheeks flare brightly, but you try to hide it.

The nurse fidgets, scratches at her sleeve. 'We're um ... he's ah ... kind of gone missing.'

Kind of gone missing.

That's exactly what she said.

You act as though everything is under control. You walk in careful, measured steps.

You tell me not to panic.

You tell me not to run.

But every room and corridor looks exactly the same – the beige carpet, cream walls and lurid eighties artwork.

Down the lift?

Outside?

Do you really think he—?

'Found him!' A bony nurse announces her prize from down the corridor. She has the brittle eyes of a first-year, gripping the back of his starched white gown firmly in her fist.

You whisper to me, out the side of your mouth – *she mustn't like the look of his arse*. You can joke now, as though everything will be okay.

He's smiling, of course. Not a worry in the whole-wide-world. And his hair stands up like the sulphured crest of a startled cockatoo.

You said once that it's just as well he's like that – happy, I mean. The doctor told me that too – some of them get really depressed. That's what they say on the Internet as well. You showed me what it said on your computer, remember? That if they realise what's happening, it's so much worse.

So we both agree, don't we? He's better off this way.

The nurse releases him into our custody.

'He was in one of the other rooms,' she says, lip twitching. 'Annoying all the patients.'

You force a smile, but it doesn't reach your eyes. 'Dad,' you say, taking his arm, 'where were you going?'

He looks at you like you are from outer space, but you pretend not to notice.

'I don't know,' he says. 'Do you?'

You called him the cliché of a migrant success story. You always had the right words. You said his self-belief was forged in those places where good intentions meet hard reality.

You said it at your wedding, remember? He really loved that day. He always loved the things you said.

But now you say he's different. A shadow of who he was. But I know that isn't true.

We all can see what's happening – it's impossible to miss. He pours wine on his breakfast cereal. Answers the phone with the remote control. Forgets which house is ours.

And I dress him in the morning, hold his hand as we cross the street, and wipe his backside in the toilets.

A lot to ask for $121.70 a fortnight, you say.

And you're probably right about that.

But you're wrong to say he's different. He's not a shadow of who he was. He's someone else entirely.

You lead him back to bed, his skin so thin you say it feels like tissue paper.

There are deep, heaving sobs from the cubicle opposite. We watch the sudden movement behind the curtain, like a shadow puppets on meth. That's how you describe it, but I don't know what you mean.

The bony nurse rushes in.

'What's the matter, Kristy?'

'The voices,' Kristy says. 'They won't stop.'

'What are the voices saying?'

'They keep telling me to cut.'

Your dad sits up in bed, narrow eyes ablaze. 'What's wrong with her?'

You place a hand gently on his chest, not knowing how to answer. 'Just keep quiet, right?'

'She should bloody keep quiet!' He glares at us like strangers. 'Where the hell's your mother?'

'She'll be back soon,' you say. 'She's busy.'

We've always been busy.

We landed first in Freo, then took the train to Melbourne. Carlton to be exact. We taught ourselves some English on the way.

A train driver, that's what he was at first. Then a publican. Then a farmer.

For a while, he was all three at once.

Jobs landed in your mailbox back then. You could take your pick. The whole world was yours, they said, if you worked hard enough.

The future? It would look after itself.

I started at a fruit can factory, Hawthorn I think it was. A winter walk and a train ride, all before the sun.

One day a milkman with sparkling eyes offered me a lift to the station.

Your dad was very interested when I told him.

He drove me to the factory every day after that.

Picked me up as well.

2. Four days ago.

You try to convince the nurse to let me stay the night.

'It's against policy,' she says. 'We only let family stay when ...'

You cross your arms. 'When what?'

'When they're ...' she whispers, like it's a secret I shouldn't be hearing. 'When they're *dying*.'

You smile. 'A bit late then isn't it?'

She says they have far worse than him.

You tell her if I can't stay, we'll have to take him home.

You look at me. I can see your thoughts. *How did it come to this?*

When she leaves, I say it. 'Do you think it's my fault?'

You look at the telly when you answer. 'I dunno, Mum. But you should try to keep the heaters on. Maybe it was the cold ...'

I dunno, Mum.

That's exactly what you said.

First, he taught himself to lay bricks. Then he built our home.

A two-storey fortress of double clinker and Spanish arches. White concrete balustrades and black ceramic tiles.

Remember how it looked, beside all those little weatherboards? How grand and proud it was? How you bashed the kids who teased you for it?

We pretended not to know about the fights. But your dad, he fought hard for us, so he didn't mind if you fought too.

Then he did his back. He couldn't drive the train after that. Couldn't handle all the shunting.

So he bought the pub in Stawell. Got it cheap. And we got to run our own show.

We poured money into the place. And you boys spent it on cars and girls. I never blame you though.

At night, I would crawl upstairs to bed. I know you saw me once. You saw my legs, all varicose and ulcers, crawling like an animal.

You and me were different after that. You think I didn't notice. Something harder in your eyes.

But we never ever talk about it.

3. Three days ago.

A small Vietnamese man is wheeled into the room. Fashionable jeans. Bright t-shirt. Bare feet with dirty soles.

'He's okay.' The nurses whisper to each other. '*Voluntary.*'

He sits quietly on his bed. Breathing deeply in and out. His thick black hair wild and bold like a proud lion's mane.

After gathering his thoughts, he inches slowly to the edge. Dangles his legs. Then screams it out.

'*Dirty... Fucking... Cunts!*'

It is incredibly loud. And I don't like that sort of language. But I think he'd have a really good singing voice, if he put his mind to it.

Your dad stares at the telly like he didn't even hear it. That *QI* show is on, but there's no sound working. I never liked that show. I go to the tearoom and eat cold spaghetti from a plastic container, standing over the kitchen sink.

A nurse seizes the moment. She goes to you and looks deep inside your eyes.

'Are you amazed at how strong she is?' she says.

'Who?'

'Your mum.'

'Dunno,' you shrug. 'Never really thought about it.'

I come back. You tell me what she said.

'What choice have I got?' I say, but I can't tell if you're listening. You're watching Stephen Fry on the telly. 'And it's not all bad.'

'Really?' you say.

I try to smile. 'I can call him *cornuto*, *cretino* and *ritardato*. Five minutes later, he's forgotten all about it.'

Later that night, while you're asleep at home, I drag your dad away from Kristy's bed – away from Kristy the cutter.

He yells at her, '*Porco Puttana!*'

The next day I tell you, but I say that it was okay. That she couldn't understand Italian.

4. Two days ago.

We take him back home.

But first, the social workers come to visit. All lined up. The best help no money can buy.

Community groups. Respite. Counselling.

You try to persuade me too. That it could be helpful. But I think it's all just rubbish.

'No,' I say. 'For now, I can cope.'

You tell them you will come around more often, but you don't look at me when you say it.

We're back at home. You sit at the table. Turn on the telly.

He goes to the toilet out back.

'Eventually,' you say, your eyes on *60 Minutes*, 'we'll have to do something.'

I tell you it will kill him.

'There's nice places. The Italian joint on Rathdowne Street.'

I tell you we can't afford it.

'So what's the plan?' you say. 'For the future?'

The future will look after itself.

'So what happens when...'

No-one can answer that.

The local coppers were trying to kill him. At least that's what he thought. They didn't like wogs in town, especially running a pub. They were trying to shut him down. Like they thought he was Robert Trimbole. You don't remember him, but he was in the mafia.

But they didn't get him in the end.

A burst blood vessel in his brain. I know you remember that. It got him deep down inside his skull.

And it got him very bad.

5. Yesterday.

He goes missing.

It was while I was doing the shopping. I came back to the door wide open, the house empty. The telly still on.

You tell me to call the police.

They're different now. But just as helpful.

'Yeah?'

'We can't find him. My husband.'

'We'll keep an eye out.'

We search the city. Fitzroy. Collingwood. Carlton. We know he'll ride the trams. Still likes the squeal of wheels on rail.

You try to act all calm, but I can tell you are upset. You keep scratching at your cheeks. Then your neck.

The skin is red.

And I can feel the edges fraying.

So I try to hold the middle.

6. Four hours ago.

It's almost dark again.

It rings and we both freeze – the sudden God of the telephone.

That's what you call it later.

You always have the right words.

You answer. You almost smile. And hang up the phone.

You tell me it's your wife.

She's found him.

She's bringing him home.

You warn me not to tell him off. Like that's the important thing right now.

'Why?' I say.

'I read it somewhere.'

I think that's meant for dogs who run away, but I don't say anything.

She brings him down the hallway and sits him in the kitchen. You both talk like he isn't there. Like I'm not there as well.

Your wife says he was in Lygon Street.

Standing outside the pasta shop.

Caught in a crowd of tourists.

A smile on his face.

He stared into the window with cloudy eyes.

Somewhere. Nowhere.

All at once.

She walked up slowly. Watched his face in dim reflection. And touched his hand just lightly.

> 'Tom, it's me. Do you know where you are?'
>
> 'No.' He shook his head. 'Do you?'

I look at him. He looks at me. And I think he knows.

Under the table, out of your sight, I squeeze his hand.

Flying to Eritrea

Jeremy Clarke

Jeremy Clarke is a writer who has previously worked as a foreign correspondent for nine years. His time was predominately spent in East Africa and the following article is a non-fiction account of one of his experiences.

I sat in a window seat on Eritrea's only commercial aircraft, weighed down by my recent memory of this very journey, one I had promised myself I would never make again.

The same battered overhead lockers rattled and swung open, ignored by the staff. The seats still pockmarked with cigarette burns, the heavy purple curtains that I yanked across the window still stained a greasy brown. The same uneasy glances stolen among the handful of inexplicable passengers, the grim resignation of a tired cabin crew, the same nausea that turned my stomach to liquid and the unmistakably chemical taint of cheap Kenyan cigarettes under my fingernails. Again, the unfocussed memory of a Nairobi farewell party that climaxed only hours ago.

Below our shuddering 747 an arid north African desert crawled along, empty hot spaces in which wreckage would take days to find.

Last September should have been my only visit to Eritrea. I knew that before I boarded the plane in these first few days of 2010. My return was resoundingly unethical, and every superstition I had told me I was moving toward the wrong place at the wrong time. Any sense this visit would be different disappeared once I boarded: it was all exactly as it had been; as it would no doubt be once we landed.

In fact, I could think of only two differences at all: the government now openly despised me and routinely ran hateful and wildly falsified opinion about me in the state press; and this time, I was smuggling in approximately three-and-a-half thousand dollars in US currency that was at this moment taped around my penis.

Eritrea's government had extended me a first and now second invitation to report from their country for only one reason, I knew that much. This was a deeply paranoid government and what they craved was to be ignored. Yet they had of late gained unwanted notoriety thanks to a list published annually by the advocacy group Reporters Without Borders: "The World's Worst Press Abusers Index". For two years in a row Eritrea had pushed North Korea into second place and people were beginning to ask, What is this country no one has heard of that is outpacing the undemocratic abuses of North Korea, our established short-hand for weird tyranny?

The last foreign journalist stationed here was expelled in 2008. I was invited to report from the capital, Asmara, in September 2009. The government's objective for my presence was to allow Eritrea to fall into the relative obscurity of second place or lower on that list, meanwhile they would make reporting in a conventional sense almost impossible; following me around, offering only rare and cryptic statements to a press corps of one, and refusing any travel requests I made to leave the tiny capital that was surrounded my military checkpoints.

This much was correctly predicted by the British ambassador during my first week in the country. She invited me over for a lunch of what she called "Australian delicacies" – in this country she was my ambassador too and was reaching out in concern or responsibility (or perhaps she felt bad for having misplaced the flak jacket, helmet and satellite phone stashed in her embassy by my predecessor with instructions to "give these to whoever gets in next").

Over white fish garnished with finely sliced lime she asked me pointedly how I ethically justified being in Eritrea, as I would in no way be able to do meaningful reporting, while helping a totalitarian government with a timely favour: conferring the appearance of "opening up"?

I had no good answer for her. She handed me a map with directions to her residence and said, "If it goes wrong, try to get inside these walls".

Returning to Eritrea now was a mistake; I still had no adequate answer for the ambassador. I was twenty-six – old enough to know I needed an answer more honourable than career and curiosity. Instead, I reasoned hopefully and a little self-importantly, any outsider's observation of this extraordinary place had value.

Or did I just want to be back there? In Asmara: the most surreal of forgotten cities. Its current incarnation of Art Deco treasures was built in a few mad years by Mussolini, and protected from ugly development by the long war with Ethiopia. It had at last begun to decay and crumble: the fading pastel colours of the Riviera. So too its beautiful mosques and cathedrals – representing two of Eritrea's four legal religions.

Eritrea's government barely trades with its neighbours, such is its commitment to a message of self-sufficiency and its presumption of international conspiracy against it, so down at the steel works at dusk you see young women of staggering beauty wearing blue boiler-suits flecked with luminescent chilli and turmeric from the nearby markets, welding away at old pieces of Soviet tank or mortar shrapnel – a rare source of reusable metal – working them into items like scissors and hair combs.

I had one of these combs stored safely in another country, the serial number of the original bomb engraved down its handle. It was made by a girl who had to disappear like so many of her compatriots: fleeing in their thousands from Eritrea's perpetual national service, constant war footing and the relentless utopian fantasies of its state press, across the border in search of unsafe boats to ferry them to Europe, or captured en route and sent to desert prisons to rot, or shot on sight.

And I only saw static, peaceful Asmara, where you might glimpse the quiet horror that rots the country but never know the unseen Eritrea, the 99 percent of its landmass that you need impossible travel permits to observe, parts of country that must tell a more urgent story. An official for a rare foreign aid agency to be permitted in the country told me of starving Eritreans staggering into their outposts from areas off-limits to aid. This official said that even in a good harvest year not enough food could be produced under its anti-trade government to adequately feed the population. And harvests across the whole region had been suffering, though the state television ran nightly reports on the bumper crop the country was again revelling in.

I had asked President Isaias Afwerki why so many of the country's youth risked their lives to flee into the unknown rather than stay and share in his vision. He had beamed at me with his lopsided smile and hardening eyes (his handlers reacting to this expression with unveiled horror), and said in an even voice, "They are just going for a picnic, I'm sure they will be back soon."

Locked on board the plane, I knew this return visit was on borrowed time. My hope was that I would be expelled with great fanfare as soon as possible; my fear was of something quite different: indefinite detention – perhaps on vague charges of terrorism? – or just a casual accident at the hands of these former freedom fighters. I didn't think that likely, but I was the only journalist to arrive for a while, there was very little on which to build intuition.

These thoughts shook me, and my roll of hundred dollar bills and the duct tape that secured them in place pinched painfully as I squirmed in my seat. (The foreign cash would be worth four or five times as much if I didn't have it tracked by the government upon arrival). I wanted to push all these thoughts into the near future where they belonged, but I preferred them to the concern of my immediate present: this terrible plane. It was technically Eritrea's national carrier, a fleet of one, under-serviced and unfit, an aircraft sometimes spontaneously commandeered by the president to fly to Qatar for purposes I had little clue about. Money? Peace talks so shameful as to be kept entirely under wraps? Medical treatment?

Before I first interviewed the president, an American official had pulled me aside to describe the various physical symptoms of this and that disease that they hoped he might have, inviting politely that I share with them any such observations. It seemed a benign request and I needed their insights to shake stories from this fortress. (Another foreign official later told me that such was the lack of international interest in Eritrea that their hunt for its notorious desert prisons sometimes amounted to refreshing Google Maps).

The president had looked strong throughout our two-and-a-half hour interview (which to my great consternation he felt successful enough to replay for many days on Eritrea's only television channel, which saw me spat on by one dissident for wasting an opportunity to expose him, yet thrown from a taxi by its driver once he recognised me, appalled by the temerity of my stronger questions). Afwerki had arrived by helicopter to where I waited in the open by two chairs and a single glass of water (I didn't touch it and nor did he); wild horses circled beyond a tight perimeter of heavily armed, war-ready guards, adding to the otherworldliness of the occasion.

The president showed no apparent symptoms of degenerative disease, as I had told my contact. The information I hoped this person would soon share could prove my justification for returning. In fact, it began a series of leaks that amount to what I would come to think of as my only successful reporting from Eritrea, even though it would lead to my unwelcome designation as a protected source in a diplomatic cable sent from the US embassy to Washington – something I would never agree to and only learn about much later thanks to Wikileaks. Like so much else about my six months in Eritrea, my incredulity may confirm a fear: I was ill-equipped to be the only foreign journalist living inside the "world's worst press abuser".

I opened the purple curtains once more and looked to the east. Asmara sits more than two kilometres above sea level. The nearest water is its Red Sea coast – the bane of landlocked Ethiopia, a coastline I was never permitted to visit. I had routinely taken a meaningless travel request to the Ministry of Information, that huge monolith on the mountain's rim whose shadow spreads wide across the city; headquarters to the country's only legal media. Not that there was any illegal media left, for the dissidents had largely fled. It was "a protest of feet", as one exile had put it to me.

Between the shaking plane and that pristine Red Sea coast with its pirates and exotic fish – which I knew would again be off-limits to me – was the Danakil Depression, the hottest place on the surface of the earth.

How could such a country exist and not be talked about? Or could it only go on existing this way because it was not talked about?

On first arrival it had felt like stepping into the yellowed pages of my high school history textbooks. I wanted to make people agree that Eritrea was unlike other parts of the world we might describe as reminiscent of Stalin's Russia, say, or similarly redolent of some mid-century culture with Orwellian dimensions – this country was firmly of that time. It was not a reimagining or an explicable extension of those societies, it was a Soviet command-economy with requisite KGB and a dictator of Bond-villain proportions, all preserved as though in amber – yet with a capital inside a mountain crater above the clouds in a forgotten corner of the world.

And unlike old communist Europe there was nothing grey about it, nor was its first sacrifice feminine beauty, as Robert Hughes had written of such arrangements of government. Pink and orange Modernist architectural gems line the sun-streaked alleyways of Asmara, where a population of overwhelming natural beauty and hard-won defiance has been whittled down to just a few broad contingents: those veterans of "The Struggle" (the guerrilla war for independence: one of the bravest and most honourable fights in the history of conflict); those young fanatics who insist their president is almost a God; and those others, plotting desperately for departure, ready to risk their lives, under pain of death, in flight, to be anywhere else at all.

It is a city and a situation that cannot endure indefinitely, or indeed for much longer. Its economy is dead and buried, throngs of its rural population are fleeing or starving, its president – Eritrea's only leader since independence – is aging. The breaking point is unknown but near. There was an attempted coup in 2013 by a general who knew he couldn't win but decided to pit himself against the logjam.

Might it be a coup then, or perhaps there will be an eventual appeal for adequate aid, thereby inviting development, decadence; the UN circus of paperwork and playboys? Will landlocked Ethiopia and its population of 80 million make another attempt on the thin sliver of coastline that is Eritrea? Will another dictator step in and what might be the nature of his lunacy – an ostentatious Gaddafi, a psychotic Amin, a racially-cleansing Bashir, a sexually depraved Mobutu? They each ruled larger countries than Eritrea in this eastern chunk of Africa.

Or what if attempts are made at internationally-led, multi-party democracy, with its decades of dirty teething, when corruption and nepotism invariably rule?

The end of post-independence-era Eritrea is unknown but looming; an Eritrea so unlike anywhere else on earth that its truth often sounds barely credible.

The Origin of Monsters

Jack Granath

On hearing the report of a black bear
Who swam with mouth wide open like a whale,
Thus catching insects, Darwin posited,
With food enough and few competitors,
The gradual development of monsters,
Which, though he did not name them, must be named
Whale-bears. Leviathan with teeth and hair.
A speculative sequel to *Moby Dick*:
The great-clawed creature rises from the water
To stalk the land, all sixty tons of him.
Ahab, weighted down with heavy skins,
Tracks him by his fluke-prints in the snow.
Close calls and agonizing disappointments
Thread through the epic, elemental chase
Until a final confrontation where
The whale-bear decimates a city block,
Which caves in on old Ahab's lighted house,
And Ishmael runs off yakking through the woods
To tell his tale. Before it comes to that
Let's heed the insight of the native child
Who hid and watched or could have hid and watched
And spoke or sang these words or some such words
In a language never translated, now lost:
"But Mr. D., that bear was only playing."

Eira

Ann Matthews

Iesu Grist, everyone including mam was right – it's bloody freezing up here in Newcastle. It's not like I don't know bout the cold, right? At home the wind and rain comes raging off Caernarfon Bay straight through your coat and jumper and BAP against your skin. And I'm no wimp, but my hands are hurting even though I've stuffed them under my T-shirt and I almost want to cry when Tiff suggests legging it home.

'Fock that.' I say.

'Come on yis lazy cow. What's the hurry?' Tiff says, shoving me with her elbow.

Tight bitch won't fork out for a taxi. Duw, I don't blame her – it's daylight robbery alright. It's gone two a.m. Anyone in their right mind, yeah, will be tucked up in bed with a hot water bottle and thick socks, head under the covers. All the sweat from being crammed in the nightclub's gone all bloody icy between my top and my skin. Tiff shows me her thermals right there in the middle of the street. How she can dance all night in them I can't imagine, but she did. Tiff's gotta theory that when you're pissed, right, you keep warm. There's men in T-shirts standing there – real men with muscles and tidy hair, an-all-that, looking at us and laffing. So I follow her towards the station. Had no bloody choice did I? Anyway it's busy like Piccadilly Circus or something – everyone falling out of the clubs and pubs and shouting over taxis and having quick fags outside the station before they catch trains or the Metro or whatever it is they're doing. We're arguing bout this and then bout that. Neither of us saying the right thing. Now we're arguing bout the best way to Byker. I know one way and she isn't coming that way. Bein a soft cow I give in, yeah really.

'I can smell snow.' I tell her.

'Don't be soft Eira – snow don't smell.' It does right. We're heading down Mosley Street. I step over a puddle of puke and Tiff just walks straight through it.

'Tiff look at your focking shoes.' She stamps her feet thinking that it'll dislodge all the bits and frowns.

'I'm not going through that underpass. No ways.'

'Why?' I ask. 'It's all lit up nice, cariad.'

Tiff stops and faces me. 'Stop calling me cari-whatever-it-is. And I'm not going that-a-way.' She starts listing a litany of abuses that have occurred to her in subways. Unbelievable yeah, one after the other and another. And the wind's coming at us down the street, driving like icicles. She heads off up Grey Street and I run to catch up. It's crowded like in the day, people window shopping, like literally, outside H & M yeah, and people eyeing up the talent too. There's loads of pissheads sitting round the monument, smoking, kissing, falling over, shouting like there's no tomorrow. Tiff's up ahead and talking to someone. I knew it... Tiff wants company – non-stop – like company is crack cocaine or something, yeah, that addictive... and here's me with an interview in the morning and no key to her place. I'm lingering, waiting for the bloody hugs to stop, jumping from one foot to the other – like you do when it's minus whatever.

They've gathered to go down the sewers or something. Anyway it isn't making any sense, right? We're off walking back the way we came – bout six of us. No idea where we're heading. I ask why we're going to see some sewers.

'They ain't sewers silly,' some girl in wellies and flowery coat laffs at me.

'Shelters.' Tiff joins in. 'Victoria Tunnel, old underground tracks from the mines to the river. A bit of local history for yis.' I shrug. Welly girl walks backwards so she can talk to me, yeah, all keen to explain it all.

'If we get nuked or come under chemical attack we should be able to use them and we can't because...' she pauses for great effect, 'they're a tourist attraction – making someone some big money somewhere we don't get a peep of. They are ours and the way things are going in the Ukraine we might need them...' Duw, she shouts things so loud I'm fully awake and paying attention. '... with all these bombs and riots and planes falling out of the sky we need to liberate what is ours in this time of need.' Haven't heard anything this lefty since my mam got pissed at her friend's funeral. Welly's got the same tight note in her voice, right – the one that's verging on the self-righteous, religious like. Tiff's just standing there nodding. Little sharp flakes of snow are piercing my skin. 'See,' Welly girl says, 'It's all going wrong, isn't it Tiffany? We don't know what will happen next. Snow in April, sheep dropping dead on the hill farms, the Tyne freezing over.'

Tiff stops walking. 'Ida, it's February and the Tyne hasn't frozen, you fool. Come here.' And Tiff gives Welly girl a big hug.

'Could do.' Welly girl answers coyly.

We're zigzagging street by alleyway, Tiff and Welly are nattering non-stop, having a mighty happy catch up. Tiff's all beaming smiles, looking beautiful, all soft focus in the street light and snowflakes. They start bounding up a big flight of concrete steps together like they're focking synchronised swimmers – me trailing ages behind.

'Give me your keys Tiff – I'm out of here.' I shout. Tiff and Welly girl laff. One of the others, a girl who looks too young to be out this late, takes my arm. I can see her neat white teeth when she smiles at me – her long wet hair brushes against my face, it smells nice, really, of roses, well something timeless and flowery, right?

Someone shouts, 'Come on.'

Everywhere we go ends in a dead end car park. No way through. It's pitch black, like before they had electricity except it's snowing properly now so it's either black or, if you look up, white. I walk along with the girl. The snowflakes melt the moment they touch us. Drops form on the fine strands of her straight black hair and slowly drip on to her coat and mine too. I ask if she's warm enough and she says she's fine. I ask her name.

She says, 'Niamh,' and spells it out for me. I tell her it's a good Celtic name. I tell her mine. 'What does it mean?' She asks.

I say, 'Snow.' We both laugh.

'Well hello snow, I'm brightness!'

Welly girl's up ahead now, an amazon warrior, leading us fock knows where. We're at that roundabout – the one with the radio station in the middle – there's taxis zooming around, like really fast in the slush. We run across slip-roads and squeeze past crash-barriers at full pelt until we're breathless. We're heading towards Byker. I'm cheering up a little, yeah, a right homing pigeon I am. The snow's sticking on the pavements and we take shelter under the railway bridge. Welly gets out a scrawled scrap of a map.

'It's definitely at the farm – next to it I'm sure.'

'Have you been there before?' Niamh asks and winks at me.

'Well sort of.'

I pipe up, 'What do you mean sort of?'

Tiff elbows me violently 'Shhhh! Do you want a bit of fun or not?' A train trundles over so I don't need to answer. That's Tiff all-over, at the moment at the least, fun fun fun. Duw, it's not that I'm against having a laff, right. It's like she's so bored she's hurtling head-on into bloody oblivion. AND isn't talking bout it neither.

'You Ok?' Niamh asks. I nod in the darkness. We're veering off onto a narrow back road, blank new flats on both sides. 'You don't live here, in Newcastle?'

'No, I used to and might again soon. And you?' She's right alongside me. She's much smaller than me, delicate like, even in a puffa jacket.

'Been here a while. You moving back to be with Tiff? She mentions you a lot.'

'We go back a long way,' I say. 'But no, I don't think so. I've got an interview up in the Children's Hospital – trying to promote myself.'

There's traffic – night buses splashing us with snowy filth.

'Down here, we're almost there!' Welly calls.

We follow – trudging downhill on virgin snow.

Tiff nudges me. 'If you had gone home you'd have missed the snow – its grand isn't it?' Then she pelts me with a snowball. Iesu Grist, next thing I know is that we're all chucking snow at each other – we're running around sweeping armfuls off all the cars, right? We're following the railway line that's way above us ducking and diving under mega high brick archways, lobbing slush balls and making a racket. Welly stops in the middle of the road and raises her arms.

'Come on folks, let's get a move on!' A slush ball hits her square on the head and everyone's laffing. We fall in line and follow her like bloody ducklings.

It's gone really quiet, everyone's shushing everyone else and slipping and sliding bout. Gotta keep the noise down, yeah. Gotta understand 'there's a job to be done.' There's some confusion. There's talk about manholes and crowbars but I'm too puffed out to even listen. I can hear animals shuffling about, snorting and a sweet warm smell coming from some building behind the fence.

'It's a bloody farm,' I say under my breath. I'm shushed. I whisper, 'What's this to do with a tunnel?' They're all walking around looking for something. Welly tries scaling a wall. A lad in combats and big boots brandishing a crowbar runs up breathless, mouthing something or other. I'm not sure if he's bloody mute or just afraid to raise his voice. Tiff, Welly and the other lad gather around him and get out the map. They turn it this way and that. And off they go. Niamh and I lean against the wall and look at the mess they've made in the snow – footprints everywhere including ours. Well I think, if they really are up to no good then here's the focking evidence, right?

'If the snow don't melt, all they have to do is photograph the soles of our shoes,' I say. We sweep our feet through all the prints, losing our balance and grabbing on to each other so we don't fall over. I'm satisfied for a minute and then realise that our prints go back, way back, for miles. We're contemplating this dilemma, and other stuff, when Tiff appears.

'Yis soft cow, standing there in tha cold.' Tiff doesn't look at Niamh, just me. Niamh takes her hand from around my shoulder, tucks her hair cutely behind her ears and says.

'Sorry Tiff,' and walks off.

'What's that bout?' I ask.

Tiff just yackers on. 'They've found it... but yis can't get in... can't budge the manhole cover... they're putting up banners... it's not criminal is it, tying banners up?'

'Does that mean we can go home now?'

'Soon. Yi killjoy, Come on!'

Welly girl has managed to climb up some metal shutters and is trying to tie up the top corners of a whopping big sheet. Niamh and the others are tugging at it, trying to fix it with string and Gaffa tape. Duw, they've spray-painted the brick walls – all untidy dripping into the whiteness. I can make out one phrase and then see that it's repeated over and over: *She who shouts loudest... will always be heard*. It's like I get all mesmerised, standing, watching, with the cold numbing me through and making me sleepy. I jump out of my bloody skin cos a wailing starts right there next to my ears, just where I'm standing, right, and before I know it everyone is scarpering. There's a blue light flashing, reflecting off the buildings at the top end of the street and coming nearer. Tiff grabs me and we run. We pass the pub and race down a path under more brick arches. I look round for Niamh but can't see her.

'Wait yis bastards.' Tiff calls out. I can't see anyone or anything. We're holding hands and running, my cariad and me. We run yeah, for ever, dizzy out of breath, lungs fit for bursting, tripping over the rough ground, under a road on stilts, through some bushes and trees and along a metal fence.

'Can yis climb this sodding thing?' Tiff asks, sliding back down to the ground.

'No!' We follow it to the right, but there's a river. We retrace our steps.

'Why are we running?' I shout in panic.

'Cos the poliss will get us – I can't hear anything mind.' We pause. It's all quiet except for the sound of cars and the wind in the trees. We huddle up right there, sitting in the snow, listening.

•

I open my eyes, not knowing where I am, right. Or why I'm stiff and so bloody cold and wet or what the hell the warm weight is leaning on me.

'Shit, Tiff!' I'm wide awake and trying to move.

'What?' She replies sleepily.

'Wake up!'

It doesn't take long and we're freaked out and up on our feet, ferreting around for our mobiles, seeing what time it is. Duw, it's five thirty bloody five and we're on the edge of having frostbite. We follow the fence – we're only seconds from civilisation. It's a blur from there, getting our bearings, walking the wrong way through places not even Tiff has been to. We end up passing the archways down Stepney Bank – the banner is half pulled down. Tiff drags me on.

It's all slushy underfoot. The snow's stopped and the sky's all mottled grey – like the dawn's trying to come, yeah, but can't quite be bothered doing its stuff. I nudge Tiff and point at a hoarding next to the building on the corner of the street: 'Newcastle's Hidden Heritage' it says, and there's a map, a plan of the tunnel.

'Oh well, whatever.' Tiff shrugs. I walk over to a door and rattle it.

'A crowbar would have done it.' I say. Tiff just drags me by the elbow and marches me eastward.

We don't speak until we're well on our way. She doesn't quite know what the hell Welly girl and the others were up to, right, and is too tired to explain anything. But I badger her, cos to me it was all a bit bout nothing.

'I know bout protests,' I say, 'Fighting for real stuff, like for housing for locals, stopping the bastards building new nuclear power stations. So what's so important bout the tunnel then?'

Tiff shrugs and yawns. 'How should I know?'

'So what were we doing then?' I say rattily, cos I'm knackered. I plonk myself on some garden wall and a dog starts barking somewhere close. She turns and faces me.

'We was just having a bit of fun, pet.' She says limply.

'Oh' I say, and add, 'Niamh's nice isn't she?'

Tiff shrugs. 'Trouble if yis asking me.' She kicks a coke can into the gutter. 'Her and her Jonty been round-about a-while, quite the item, pet, til he was banged up for something or other.'

'Oh.' I say. 'And Welly girl?'

'What about Ida?'

'Didn't take to her. So I suppose that means she's dead nice, right?'

'Right.'

'Is that all you've got to say?'

Tiff shrugs. 'None-of yis business.'

'Oh' I say. 'It's like that is it?'

'What is?'

'You and Ida?'

'Maybe. Maybe not. Life's too short to get tied down like that.'

'You've changed your tune.'

'Well, yis no fun.'

'Cheers. You told me bout the bloody job – you said Go for it, perfect job for you, so I reckon you could be a bit more understanding bout it. I've gotta look responsible right? There's drugs tests, police checks. I'm trying not to fock it up... I thought you wanted me to move back up.'

'Yis used to be a right laugh, tha's the Eira I liked. The one who stayed up all night singing me songs. Life and soul of the party.' I get up and see my bedraggled outline in a car window and make an attempt to straighten my crumpled coat and flatten my hair. I bend to look at my neon reflection in a wing-mirror and wipe my eyes with the cuffs of my coat sleeves.

'Yis coming or not,' Tiff calls.

'Suppose so.' I mumble. I bang roughly into the car, the headlights start flashing and the alarm starts screaming ee ooo ee ooo. We cover our ears and leg it down the street.

Birthday

Mary Petralia

I said thank you God
and almost believed it,

then a woman in a riot stole
toilet paper and paper towels

instead of a TV or cell phones
and a radio DJ made fun of her;

you cretin, paper products
aren't a benefit of SNAP

plus you don't even know
how to pronounce "judgmental."

But really it's not so much that I want
to preach to the choir

it's just that I hope there is a choir
and it doesn't necessarily have to sing

but more, hear, and it would be good
if the choir knew what it was like to be on food
stamps.

BIRTHDAY

I don't blame her for stealing
those things,

I've done it; taken toilet
paper rolls from the beach bathroom.

A woman in a park
swung her dead child for three nights.

I stay up till midnight
to instantly win a new grill

but what I really want is the free
trip to Hawaii.

I love Hawaiian rolls,
they're so darn sweet.

I hear Hawaii is no paradise,
the flying cockroaches,

but that flowery blue ginger
is like a purple heaven-bird.

I had a patient from Palau and that chick
was nuts but sweet like an Almond Joy.

The Pacific must do something
to create some chaos effect.

Maybe it's floating radiation.
Maybe it's crawling disappearances.

Maybe they just want their spoons
to not tarnish so quickly.

My daughter is upset because she didn't get a picture
of the prison's pristine garden as we drove by.

Sometimes we see basketball players in the yard,
nuclear white in uniform.

All it takes is one person
to describe you as mediocre.

You lie still and dull-colored
and think of that squealing skinned-alive rabbit.

Lie still and remember the way the Italian pines
shushed and curtained just for you

because you were only Italian back then and the fortresses
you built were in your backyard and not in your mind.

Peel off a vegetable's vitamin skin,
your stone-thrown Medusa

snake hair only gray and soft wires.
Peel off another month

on a Japanese woodblock-print calendar.
Cherries still blossom. Warriors float.

Dead Mothers and our Fathers

Tanushree Baidya

I called Mrinal, "M," for no spectacular reason and just so. M was intrinsically a whiner. Her purpose in life remained elusive she claimed. She was always unhappy, always complaining. She struggled through all she did, simply because she had no heart in it, she explained. At times, she made us wonder about our lives too, to question how things were going. Somehow none of us took life as seriously as M did. Her constant despondency was a bit aggravating at times. We continued with our lives and jobs, M continued hers with numerous life style problems like migraine, weight gain, depression and an idiot boyfriend. She had incredibly frizzy hair, which she could never properly style. "Why can't this one thing in my life just fall in place on its own!!!" she'd say.

She was always stressing and struggling. She was confused, and nothing she did gave her any satisfaction. She felt she would be better off doing something else, but was unable to define what that 'something else' should be. After college we all managed decent paying jobs, as did M, but she remained unsatisfied. "No, works good, it pays my bills", she often said with that constant tone of resignation. On weekends, she would take writing and art workshops, and even tried learning a foreign language. To me it was all so bizarre and I considered it simply an indulgence which many of us could not afford. That indulgence made her so much more despondent but still so much more hopeful than any of us. Once my father had remarked to my mother, "That's what happens when parents let their daughter run wild. They become like Mrinal, a vagabond." My father had never liked Mrinal.

M had this activist sort of sensibility, quick to defend, offend, take a stance and forsake on your behalf, 'your' being us, her friends, especially me. We became friends on the first day of college. She always wore stylishly cut, bright coloured, loose, kurtis over jeans, with a scarf (most often a dark navy coloured one) around her neck. On her heavy set frame the attire sat well. She was kind, affectionate, ready to put everything aside if you came looking for help. Her cynicism and constant gripe coupled with her incredible wit made for zany discussions and debates. We'd often pick on her, on her cynicism, on her 'there has to be more to life than this' syndrome, as we called it. But we respected her educated and worldly point of view. She'd had a different upbringing from us. It was more sophisticated, more evolved. She was the intellectual in our friend circle. Her parents spoke to her in English. She read fancy books, and had watched movies and shows we'd never even heard of back then. She was our group leader, educating us, introducing us to American sitcoms, Italian food and Cappuccinos. And we were grateful to her. I always found her oddly reassuring. She once said that in me she saw a person who had so much to see and experience. She called me her 'project'. I did not mind it.

The first time I had questioned my sexuality, I had discussed it with M. We were sitting on the stone steps under the banyan tree behind the college library. It was a hot summer afternoon, but cool under our beloved tree. The crows were cawing and there were squirrels everywhere waiting for crumbs. We spoke about it so objectively that it didn't feel like a life altering realization. She helped Poorva and I come out to our friends. They were appalled initially, attributing it (being gay that is) to M's influence, as if we were doing it to be cool.

I had not seen M in four years. We lost touch after her mother was murdered and she stayed back in Kolkata, where her parents had lived. I was with her when her mother had died. That terrible night. Much had happened, changed and afflicted M's life since. When she called me a week earlier to tell me that she was coming to Bombay for a conference, I felt a wave of uneasiness and guilt. Four years is a long time.

We met in a coffee shop on Carter road, Bandra, close to where my father's apartment was. She picked the place. I wondered if I would run into my father. I hadn't visited him in months. Not since after my mother had died. I remembered how he had never liked Mrinal, 'Vagabond, bad influence', his words still echoed in my mind. But from what I heard from my brother, my father was a vagabond now.

I was expecting M to be fat, forlorn, wrinkly, and with that familiar and constant look of anxiety. But here she sat looking lovely as never before. She sipped her coffee breathing in the aroma, her eyes roving, her face shimmering in the soft yellow light of the cafe, overlooking the sea. The clothes were white; the hair was silky straight, and her hand bag pink, all in harmony, so exquisite. She sat upright, shoulders thrown backwards, neck swan, a gentle heave on her breast, the soft skin peeping. There was an air of exaggerated grace around her, and so unlike her old slouchy whiney self. Oh, if only my father could see her now.

"You and Poorva still in touch?" She asked me nonchalantly, stirring her coffee. I smiled and nodded.

Her face lighted up and she asked, "How often do you guys meet. How do you manage?"

"We don't, not since after the kids. She can't afford to visit me here, and my kids are still too young for me to go see her."

M looked a little unsure, and asked, almost apologetically, "Why can't she afford a plane ticket?"

"Oh, I thought you knew. The guy she married... his business failed, and he was anyway involved in some bad things here, bad dealings. They had to leave; they are living with his parents now in Gwalior. It's this little town in Madhya Pradesh somewhere. Seriously, what were her parents thinking, marrying her off to a loser" I said and wondered if I sounded aggrieved.

"Trupthi, I know Gwalior, I lived there once. I didn't know Poorva had to move away... and this way." M said. I sensed the disappointment, not so much for Poorva, or me, but for the failure of the plan, the crazy plan.

"I got lucky with mine in a way. He does what he said he does. But then I got pregnant too soon." I said.

M laughed and said, 'Ech kids. But wow, you and Poorva actually went through with it. My idea! The set up is still perfect, maybe it'll work out." she said proudly, pouting her lips.

"You know how these things go M. She's so far away now. If you thought my father was controlling, my husband is worse. Life's changed. With kids nothing else really matters to me now anymore to be honest. I am very settled in life now." I don't know why I felt compelled to explain myself, sound like a victim again. M never asked about my kids.

I do love my kids, but I don't want M to know that. I don't tell her that Poorva had begun to feel irrelevant to my life that even though I loved her, the urges were under control. Hah!, that's what my mother had once called them, 'urges'. I had been surprised at my mother's reaction, when she'd walked in on Poorva and me kissing. The terror I had felt on seeing my mother, and then the astonishment at her calm and kind face. The calmness had disturbed me.

She had sat me down, my mother, my fingers on her palm. She did not look alarmed or confused. There was this sad smile, an understanding – where did it come from; I have never been able to comprehend. She said "I'm not saying it is wrong Trupi, we all have urges. You just need to control it to have a normal life. What can you do anyway! You have to be more careful, your father will kill you and her. You cannot do anything about it, not here."

And she was right; it wasn't really that hard controlling them now that I had to live the life my father had steered me to.

If not for M, may be I'd never have acted on those urges. And not disregarded my father as much. Normality, I'd once said, M had laughed and said, "If normality is what you seek, then you don't know your chemistry very well."

M's idea, the plan, wasn't a plan at all. My father insisted that I marry as it was time to do so. So I did, to a guy he chose. The plan for Poorva and me to manage a relationship on the side was only a consolation. But this idea of dual existence, superimposed new self wasn't for me. Poorva ended up rushing into a marriage so that we could be neighbours. Now she's rotting in a small town hating her life and here I am making peace with mine. Poorva blamed me, held me responsible for her state. But what could I do.

M had a way of dreaming up life, lives, of wanting to create little bubbles, more like ripples. So temporary. At the core she was (is) a protean being. For her the river ran deep, accumulating the mind's deepest darkest desires, notions, wants and needs as sediments on a river bed. She thrived on it, hoping it would change the course – by acting upon random fancies, chasing notions of what life ought to be. When I was younger, it had impressed me, this idea, this so called notion of being, but now it only made me mad.

"How is your father?" she asked breaking into my thoughts. *He's become a vagabond. A vagabond.*

"He is ok. After Mum died he sort of feels lost I guess. It's only been 8 months since she died, so maybe it's that. My family thinks it is probably the onset of Alzheimer's. But we are having a hard time taking him for tests. He gets aggressive. I mean he always had a temper. But this is different... I mean we, my brother and I are doing everything" I said

"How bad is it? Does he talk to you?" she asked.

When has he ever talked to me about anything!

"Not really. I mean he just does his thing, living his retired life, goes to the beach... takes his walk and stuff. My brother and I check up on him." I lied.

I could always talk to M. In college I had spent long hours telling her about my father and his rules, his obvious preference of my brother over me, his constant distrust of my actions and ambitions for no reason. She always found it baffling. I wanted to tell her more now, tell her how I never go to see him anymore because I feared him no more and that his suffering did not affect me. The one thing that bounded me to my father had been my love for my mother, but after her death that thread was lost too. But I could not say these things to M, not after all that she was going through. It would be wrong to do so.

She smiled sadly. I waited.

Then she said it "It is weird isn't it – your father, my mother." *Oh GOD*

"M, I don't think you should compare them, I mean it isn't... "

M did not let me finish and said "Relax. I am only talking about their state of mind and nothing else. Don't freak out. I think even we'll go through the same when we get old... well older, we are already old aren't we..."

We are quiet for a while. We finally talked about her mother – Namrata Guha. I used to call her Auntie Nimmi.

"Mumma wasn't very happy when dad left the army. I think the change in lifestyle sort of drove her a bit nutty too" M said.

M was the only army kid in our friend circle. Her father whom I called Jaydeep uncle was a high ranking officer in the Indian army, a General I think. Stuff she talked about, her life growing up as an army kid in army cantonments seemed a very charmed life, even though soldiers were dying every day at the border. High teas, ladies club, the May Queen Ball, the Winter Ball, Husband's night, Raising Day, War Widows Charity events, Welfare meets, these were things M's mother was always involved in, that was her life, and M said she missed it. M made it sound like this fallacious world her mother basked in. M's opinion of her mother was never very kind, she called her a snob, a hypocrite. She worshipped her father. I disagreed of course. Auntie Nimmi was wonderful. M had had a sophisticated upbringing thanks to her mother. She grew up reading her mother's books, Anna Karenina, War and Peace, Great Expectations, We the Living and Madam Bovary were some of the titles she'd gush about. Her mother had cultivated an environment where intellectual conversations and fancy food was a part of everyday life. And I couldn't even wear a knee length skirt around my father. Her mother (and father) gave M so much freedom. I think I would have turned out differently had Auntie Nimmi been my mother instead of the father that I had.

As I mentioned earlier, I hadn't really spoken to M since after the incident. The whole thing was so tragic and shocking. What does one say in a situation like this? It was unsettling to be sitting in this cafe, going over the past in my head, and talking about her family, my family. Everything was so normal, the coffee, the weather and the people present. M stood out; Did people recognize her here? Maybe not, not in this city.

Her peaceful countenance now bothered me as she carried on with her monologue. "Mumma did not like the change one bit." She said.

I was confused. She talking about her mum, about why it happened... trying to explain a situation I wondered whether she herself understood.

M continued talking, "Dad had stopped caring. You can't blame him, he had his own shit to feel bad about. Anyway he had hated leaving the army, but he said he saw no other option. He was dealing with life after the army so much better than Mumma."

M was now talking to herself. Her voice was so soft that I could barely hear her. I wasn't sure how to react. Should I ask questions, should I just nod away or simply be? Did it matter?

M continued talking, "It wasn't the best neighbourhood they moved to. It was pretty shitty actually. Four months before Mumma they had been a rape and murder in the area. Mum felt let down by

Dad. That he'd exposed her to things that her life in army had protected her from."

My discomfort increased. The act of rationalizing is often mistaken for catharsis. But was she? It was afternoon three pm. I looked out the window, the sun seemed harsh. A little girl with a baby was resting on the raised platform, just outside the coffee shop, her back to us, staring at the sea, waiting for the lights to turn red. Poor thing. For a few seconds I wondered how many cars would bother rolling down their window and let in the heat to give her something – few coins, half eaten sandwich, biscuits. I remembered the food drives M and I used to do in college. I realized with regret that I had already swallowed my sandwich.

I turned to M. She was stirring her coffee, regulating her breathing as if she was doing yoga, and then she started talking again, rather emphatically.

"Mumma often complained how men would just come into the apartment claiming to look into why the faucets were leaking, or why the toilet would overflow but never really fix anything. She'd complain how her neighbors weren't friendly, and so not the crowd she was used to. I'm not sure about people anymore Mrinu, Mumma would say." She paused and I looked at her with what I hoped was a neutral and understanding face.

M loved her father, her hero. The man she always wanted to emulate. It was sad, it really was.

"Are you okay?" I asked and held M's hand. I wanted to rub it against my face, smell her wrist, M, the pessimist, M the brooder, M, my best friend from college. The last time we'd met, her gripe on life had remained the same. And after the incident and her leaving the company we worked in, we barely spoke. It wasn't anyone's fault. We both had so much on our plate. M was ordering more food for us now. Her parents were always so very nice to me. I still remember Auntie Nimmi's sweet voice on the phone with my father, pacifying him, covering for me so many times during college, "Mr Muthusamy, don't worry. Your daughter is fine with us. They were working on some project and it got late. Now you won't be angry with her for staying with us now, will you??" My father always ended up being rude to her, but Auntie Nimmi never held it against me.

I looked away, thinking about that day when her mother had died – the screaming and all that blood. M and I were in Kolkata for an assignment and were to meet her parents for dinner that evening. M's mum was found stabbed in the abdomen. M's father, Jaydeep uncle, had found her on the living room floor, screaming and bleeding profusely he said. The murder weapon, probably a knife, was never recovered. The neighbours had heard screams, but did not make much of it, as if it was something that happened often, the screaming and shouting that is. When the ambulance arrived at the hospital, we were already at the gate. I watched Jaydeep uncle jump out the ambulance, his sleeves rolled up, his tall well-built frame slouched, his shirt was soaked with blood and sweat. I was at the entrance when Auntie Nimmi was wheeled in. The scene unfolding was familiar, right out of the movies, green doors, grey walls, white light, so very white and cold, gaunt people, the screaming and all that blood. Uncle, so tall and suddenly so grey, was speaking to the staff. M was screaming at the ward boy to be careful. It was a hot day; the humidity must have been at 90 percent. The glistening faces around, some curious, some in pain, some in a daze rudely awakened and many indifferent, streamed in and out of my focus.

The police came. The hesitation and confusion on part of the hospital was frustrating, as if the hospital had never dealt with such a situation. I was right behind M and Jaydeep uncle . We followed the doctor and nurses wheeling the bleeding Auntie Nimmi somewhere inside the emergency room. I took over the paper work from M's hand as we waited for the elevator. I still remember the eerie silence in spite of the usual hospital buzz, as the screams were no more. The moment seemed frozen, as if waiting, and suddenly M's mother's voice boomed - clear, chilling and depraved. There was no pain in it, only a lot of anger, people began gathering around. M seemed unfazed, not really comprehending, Jaydeep uncle stopped short in his tracks, his shoulders slouching, his eyes red and glaring. There was a look of great pain and disbelief. My eyes roved between the two, as M's mother's voice echoed through the hallways.

"It was you, you did this." She continued screaming, pointing at M's father.

That was four years ago. Auntie Nimmi died that evening. M roamed the hospital corridors endlessly for hours, lost; we spent all the time in the hospital. The operation had gone on for few hours, I cannot remember how long though. Police took those words as dying declaration and Jaydeep uncle was arrested. Relatives began to seep in within the next few hours. The media hounded the family for weeks after wards. I left M's side after three days.

M stayed back in Kolkata, she never came back to the company we both had worked for then. Her father's entry into the building was confirmed by the building's watchman who shared his own version of what happened with the media. None questioned the building security lapse, if any. The time difference between Jaydeep uncle's entering and rushing out of the building was found to be barely fifteen minutes. The army officials never commented on the case, but Uncle Jaydeep's clean and professional record was affirmed by the authorities. I remembered my father chuckling at the new reports, trashing M's family and our friendship. It had made me sick.

The media frenzy was sickening. 'Ex-army officer killing his wife' seemed to eclipse most local and even national news for 5 whole days. For a few weeks I followed the news item. Her father even passed the polygraph test it was reported, but the police were convinced it was him. M gave one interview and complained about the police mucking the crime scene.

Occasionally I texted M, awkward---'how's it going, can I do something' messages. She did not reply back. I got back and got married the same year, quit my job and became a house wife as my husband demanded.

"It is frustrating. The police say there is no evidence of anyone else doing it, so according to them that means Dad did it. It is bizarre. The whole system is pretty fucked up. They arrested him because they needed to show action and results. They said that dad could have gotten rid of the knife on his way to the hospital. He couldn't have. He was at the back in the ambulance, all windows were shut. They never found the murder weapon, that sort of works in our favour. Dad even passed the polygraph..." she paused, "Sorry... I always get excited talking about the case. That's my life now" M said as her hands swayed in air. My eyes swayed along.

She spoke for a while, giving me all the details of the case. I heard the words; there was pain, immutable pain which I did not doubt. But there was this positive fervour to her tone, an excitement. Mrinal, my M, looked up, looked into my face. Here we sat in a Cafe – two dead mothers, a senile father, another one in jail for murder. The coffee machine buzzed behind the counter; the pop music, barely audible, synced with the humdrum around, felt incredibly musical. I realized that M and I had been tapping our feet to the music, my left hand lay on her wrist, playing with the bracelet.

"Do you like it in Kolkata?" I asked.

She smiled, relaxing, "It is a funny city. For starters I was forced to improve my Bengali. The police are a squalid bunch, eager to please and then to disclaim."

She paused and looked at me "In the area I live in now, everyone knows my story and are quite nice to me actually. It's a good neighbourhood, safe. Dad insisted that I live there. It doesn't stop the trash talk though. I have become a sort of a tragic beauty queen there. Which under the circumstances is quite sickening... but you know I find myself keeping up appearances, a kind of façade, an affectation. Isn't that horrible?"

I chuckled. Of course M would use a word like 'affectation' to describe her state.

"It never hurts to look good. And you do look great" I couldn't help saying.

She fights for her father. The case drags on. It will take a few years she explained. M had a late evening flight back to Kolkata; she had a regular job with a market research firm as a business analyst. We discussed the three lawyers she had changed since the inception of the case, and the volume of law books she had read. She tried to explain the loopholes and how there might be hope. The murder weapon was still missing. She cribbed about crummy relatives and the over supportive ones. She said her migraines were almost cured as she sipped her fourth cup of coffee. I gushed about her weight loss and glowing skin. She looked around with an exquisite nonchalance. I sensed an odd calmness in her; maybe I was over thinking it, trying to validate her present self. I can't quite explain why but she seemed grounded, as if she finally found it. She seemed younger than me and all our friends - we are fat now, whining and always troubled, an aging bunch with baby talk and bored husbands. It bothered me, her confidence, the youthfulness, the bloom, and the maturity. It really did. These thoughts went on in circles in my head as I watched her munch into her cheesy Panini. Life seemed to have a purpose for her now and her story an uncomfortable closure. I knew I should not assume, presume, pass judgment but I could not help but wonder '*did he do it, does she know*' and she had never looked this beautiful.

Man Drowns in Cruise Ship Pool

Kevin Casey

The rich and krill-thick brine that rinses
the lungs' pink coral, and the light shafts
piercing the pearls of breath that rise
in spirals toward the mottled sun --

O, there's forty fathom or more below,
no danger there from wreck nor gale
amidst the veils of kelp. But you weren't
wrapped in an oil-skin and jumper, a clewline
trailing from your hand as you sank away
back into the arms of the cold Atlantic,
rueing this life's brief shore leave,
to live your death among the horned wrack
and sand sharks that prowl
the channel to St. George's port.

Senied that secret of the mariner's dream,
you bob back to the surface of a bright,
tiled pool, through the thin film of chlorine
that foams about your limbs as you're pulled
into the shallow end, your fellow passengers
horrified and leering, deck chairs scattered.

Still, high above, a gull rides the following wind
to guide you back north, the rudder swung hard over,
past the light that guards the ledges off Cohasset.

The Oracle at Delphi Street

Jon Etter

The agents of fate are many and varied. In this case, the agent of fate was George Rafferty's colon. A combination of a bad diet, dissatisfaction with his job as a cubicle-monkey, and the stress of a long string of bad investments had been taking a definitive and unpleasant toll on his digestive tract of late, a toll that was demanding to be paid one Wednesday evening on his ride home from work.

George squirmed uncomfortably and looked with anxiety at the list of stops above the train's door. Ten stops. Could he make it until he got home? George uncrossed and recrossed his legs. His abdomen made a burbling sound. George hugged his stomach, clenched his buttocks, and bent at the waist. His intestines seemed to lurch. He would not make it home, he concluded. He was going to have to get off at the next stop and use the station bathroom.

George staggered out of the train onto the platform of the Delphi Street station, but there was no bathroom in sight. Like many stations in the poor parts of the city, the Delphi station was stripped to a bare minimum - two stairways leading up to the train platform, a couple entry and exit turnstiles, and a commuter card dispenser, which in this case had been savagely dismantled.

I need to get out of here, George thought, but a rumbling in his abdomen told him that getting back on the train was not an option. So George stumbled through the turnstile onto Delphi Street in search of a bathroom.

The Delphi Street station belongs to one of those forsaken neighbourhoods that exist in every major city in the world: neighbourhoods where most storefronts are boarded up or covered in newspaper;

neighbourhoods where the only "legitimate" businesses that bother to set up shop offer junk food, alcohol, or pay-day loans; neighbourhoods where the streets and sidewalks—covered in cracks, holes, and half-hearted patch-up jobs—share the exhausted, wounded, desperate looks of its residents; neighbourhoods where the "good" people of the city never go, except to buy drugs or sex or anything else that can be had cheaply and at the expense of the lives of the locals; neighbourhoods where the poor, the helpless, the hopeless, the addicted, the unwanted, the outcast, and the criminal all coalesce in one convenient, easy-to-ignore mass of humanity. And this is where George Rafferty had come to take a shit.

George rushed down the street, desperately scanning the storefronts for some place that might have a public bathroom. About a half a block away, he spied a Dunkin' Donuts. He dashed past what he assumed to be a drug-deal into the store and up to the counter, where he was promptly told that they did not have a bathroom.

"Then where the hell do you go when you have to go to the bathroom?" George snapped at the woman working the register.

"I go home, which is where I suggest you take your white-ass right now," she replied, calmly drawing a wooden billy club from under the counter. George beat a hasty retreat out of the store, his abdomen grinding and his behind convulsing.

At the corner of the next block was a run-down looking gas station. Fearing that it might be too late, George broke into a sprint, slammed through the door, and desperately asked the cashier, "Do you have a bathroom?"

The cashier frowned from behind the plexi-glass. "Yeah."

"Oh, thank God!"

"Paying customers only."

George looked around, grabbed a newspaper, grabbed a twenty out of his wallet, and shoved it through the pay slot. "Here. Hurry. Where's the bathroom?"

The cashier took the ten. "Round back," he said as he slowly and methodically made change. "You'll need the key." After counting out George's change, the cashier made a show of rattling around under the counter before taking out and slowly sliding over a key attached to a small wooden plaque reading "World's Greatest Grandpa." George quickly stuffed his change into his pocket, grabbed his paper and the key, and hurried out the door.

As it turned out, no key was really necessary as the lock had been broken, possibly years ago. What was needed was a serious cleaning. The flickering fluorescent lighting revealed a bathroom long given over to the mould, mildew, and grime that coated the floor, sink, and toilet. The walls, moreover, were covered floor to ceiling with graffiti. As George struggled out of his pants and practically fell onto the toilet, he noticed that the only part of the bathroom not vandalized was a patch of white space on the back of the bathroom door about six inches by six inches above which was neatly printed: ASK A QUESTION AND MAKE AN OFFERING.

As George's body worked hard to turn itself inside out (at least that's how it felt to George), he took out the business section of the paper and started scanning the stock report, even though he checked the ticker religiously online at work and during his commute to and from work. He frowned at the paper, which seemed largely to be a tribute to his bad judgment and lousy business sense. Everything he had bought stock in recently had, at best, dropped sharply or, at worst, filed for bankruptcy. "Maybe I should start asking companies to pay me not to invest in them," George mused bitterly. "Damn it, what the hell should I invest in?"

Thoroughly emptied out, George got up and was about to flush when he noticed that the ten-dollar bill that had been part of his change for the newspaper had fallen out of his pocket and into the bowl in his haste to not soil himself. "Goddamn it," he muttered. "Like I haven't wasted enough money today!"

He briefly contemplated fishing it out but immediately thought better of it. That ten's just gone, he concluded, so he flushed, rinsed off his hands, wiped his hands on his trousers rather than the once white now deep brown "sanitary" hand cloth, and turned to leave.

As he reached for the doorknob, he noticed something odd. The spot on the door that he had thought was blank wasn't blank at all. Printed in that space (and very neatly for graffiti) were the words "Burroughs Pharmaceuticals." George was slightly perplexed. He was sure that the space was blank when he came in. This mystery, however, was quickly abandoned when George heard what he was certain were gunshots from what sounded like a block or two away. George hurried out of the bathroom into the alley behind the gas station, doing his best to avoid eye contact with the group of three rough-looking men who were shoving around and shouting profanities at what looked to be an emaciated junky.

•

The next day at work, George plodded somnambulistically through his duties, reading reports, writing reports, fact-checking reports, reviewing old reports, filing and refiling reports. While George was quite certain that somebody somewhere cared about all of these reports, he had no idea who and no idea why. All he knew was that he didn't give a damn about his job except for the paycheck and the health coverage, which was why he spent every moment he could get away with (which was quite a lot, actually) playing around on the internet. That was how he got sucked into playing the stock market.

It started simply enough. He had heard a couple guys in the breakroom talking about some internet company that was sure to take off, so he poked around on the web, checked some business and technology sites to read up on the company, and then decided to risk sixty bucks on the chance of making a little money on the deal. That afternoon he watched his investment double and then triple and then finally quadruple by the close of trading that day, and George was officially hooked.

George's addiction, unfortunately, progressed pretty much the way all addictions progress. Things were great at first, and George started contemplating quitting his soul-crushing job, but then he made a couple bad buys and lost almost everything he had made. Rather than walk away from the market or choose lower-risk investing, George kept throwing more and more money at riskier and riskier deals, steadily depleting his life's savings in the process.

And so on this fateful day, George threw down his pen on top of the stack of monthly finance reports he was sifting through, rubbed his eyes, and checked the markets for his daily fix. There it was—another testament to his failure. More bankruptcies, scandals, and reports of mismanagement from companies he had put his money in. More record profits for companies he passed on or bailed out on early. More proof that he, George Rafferty, would never live in the lap of luxury and would be stuck working at his miserable little job in his miserable little cubicle so that he could afford his miserable little apartment until the day of his miserable little death. I wonder if they still have a Potters Field for poor people, George mused. They'll probably just sell me to a medical college and dissect me like frog.

As George sifted through his fifth online business report, he remembered last night's unpleasantness and the writing on the gas station's restroom door. Burroughs Pharmaceuticals. Why would I remember that? he wondered. And why would someone write that of all things on the door of a restroom?

The words "Burroughs Pharmaceuticals" were so unshakably lodged in George's head that he couldn't think about anything else for the rest of the day. A quick Internet search revealed that Burroughs was a relatively small, locally-based research and development company that had gone public a few years ago. So far, it had produced a moderately successful sleep-aid and a drug that relieved the symptoms of a rare blood disorder, but nothing else of note. The company's future looked so unremarkable that George usually wouldn't have looked twice at it. But something in the back of his head told him to take the chance, so George invested all that was left in his back account in the company written on the back of a restroom door.

By the end of the day, George's faith in his excretory oracle had paid off, with stock gains earning him a whopping four dollars and sixteen cents. Well, George thought, I guess it's better than every other investment I've made for the past year. George decided to give it one more day and then move on to greener fields.

George discovered the next day, however, that few fields were lusher and greener for a cash cow to graze in than Burroughs Pharmaceuticals. The next morning, as George read while ignoring the stack of bi-weekly finance reports stacked on his desk, Burroughs held a press conference to announce that it had just developed an anti-depression drug three times as effective as the leading drugs on the market with what seemed to be absolutely no side effects or health risks. George watched with glee as his investment doubled and then tripled and then quadrupled until his investment was worth over twenty-times what it had started at less than a week before.

As his stock rose and rose, George thought more and more about the source of his good fortunes. Who wrote "Burroughs Pharmaceuticals" on that bathroom wall? Was it some employee who lived in the neighbourhood? A bored stockbroker with irritable bowels who had had to make an emergency stop like me? Some homeless investment savant? And were there other tips hidden in the graffiti of that bathroom? George had no idea, but he decided to go back that night to get an answer to that last question.

•

After George made his way nervously from the train to the gas station and let himself in thanks to the broken lock, he began scanning the walls of the restroom. He saw obscure gang symbols, drawings of genitals, a variety of crude words so comprehensive that there were at least three he had never seen before, but no stock tips. Then

George looked at the door and was taken aback. "ASK A QUESTION AND MAKE AN OFFERING" was right where it had been the previous week, but where "Burroughs Pharmaceuticals" had been was now just a blank space.

George couldn't understand it. Why erase or paint over one piece of graffiti (and the least offensive one at that) and leave the rest? It just doesn't make sense...

And then George thought back to that previous night in the restroom. He had thought the space was blank when he first sat down but discovered that it wasn't when he left.

He sat down again and stared at the space. It still said nothing. Then George started to think more about the statement above the space: ASK A QUESTION AND MAKE AN OFFERING. What does that mean? Ask who and offer what?

Then George remembered that he had wondered aloud about what he should invest in the last time he was there. He looked around, embarrassed, and then said quietly, "Uh, what should I invest in now?"

He stared at the blank space on the door. He waited. Nothing happened.

Then he remembered the ten that he had had to flush. Was that it? Was that the "offering" the door wanted? George chuckled at how ludicrous the whole idea of a fortune-telling toilet was.

And then he stopped chuckling and took a ten out of his wallet. Worth a shot, I suppose. "What company is going to have the biggest gains over the next week?" he asked before dropping the ten into the toilet and flushing. As it swirled its way down the drain, words began to slowly appear in the blank space on the door: Sirius Cybernetics Corporation.

George's mind reeled. He stared at the door, trying to make sense of what had just happened. He couldn't. In the end, sheer greed and the fear of physical harm trumped awe of the wondrous (as they often do), and George fled Delphi Street and went home to a sleepless night contemplating another stock windfall. Should he dump all of his Burroughs stock and gamble that on Sirius or should he just put a hundred or so in as he had before?

George decided to play it safe, but not too safe, and decided to risk a thousand on what the magic restroom had told him, a move he came to regret as Sirius stock shot up after landing a major military contract worth billions of dollars.

•

Over the course of the next several weeks, George made more and more trips to the restroom oracle of Delphi Street and more and more profits investing in whatever the door told him to. He also spent less and less time doing his actual work at his day job and tried less and less to keep up even the appearance of fulfilling his duties. When George's supervisor called him into his office to discuss his concerns about George's recent job performance, George explained he no longer needed the job, wished his supervisor well in his future as a "corporate stooge and paperwork zombie," placed a crisp hundred dollar bill on top a the pile of weekly financial reports on his boss's desk, told him to invest it in Krebstar stock and "to buy himself something pretty" with his profits from it, and then swaggered out of the office.

To celebrate his newfound freedom, George took a stroll through the park, occasionally laughing to himself about his poor, pathetic co-workers, suffering through their pathetic drudgery for a bi-weekly paycheck that was less than what he was sure he could now make in about an hour thanks to a certain door in the bad part of town. Afterwards, he enjoyed a big meal at a four-star restaurant, where he treated the staff rudely but where he tipped generously, good money being much more important than good manners, he thought. After that, it was drinks, a fine cigar, and a few passes at women who he thought would probably be much more receptive if they had any idea that they were being hit on by a future millionaire.

On the train (he really needed to get his own car) back to his little apartment (he really needed to get himself a big house), George decided to make a stop at Delphi Street before calling it an evening. After all, if the stock market was now his full-time job, he wanted to have a big first day.

The combination of anticipated wealth, expected ease, and a few too many strongly mixed drinks freed George of his usual anxiety while walking along Delphi Street. Tonight was his, and he would enjoy it. He surveyed the great ruin that was Delphi Street and thought, I could probably buy and sell everything and everyone around here five times over by the end of this year.

It was a thought that made him smile broadly as he went into the gas station and pay for a copy of the newspaper (this stop would have to be more than just fiscal business thanks to the rich meal and copious drinks) with a fifty. As the cashier began to ask him for a smaller bill, George cut him off. “Keep it,” he said with a wink, “There’s plenty more where that came from.”

With paper tucked firmly under his arm, George closed the bathroom door behind him and took a twenty out of his wallet. “Okay, what do I need to know tonight?” He dropped a twenty into the bowl, gave it a flush, and turned around. Slowly the door revealed its message: GET OUT NOW.

George stared at it. Get out now? George was puzzled. Why should I get out of the market now? I’m making hand over fist!

“Is that right? What do I need to do if I’m going to get really, disgustingly rich?” George asked as he flushed another bill.

“GET OUT NOW,” the door continued to read.

“Huh!” George said as he dropped his trousers and sat down. He still couldn’t make sense of it. He started reading through the business section of the paper looking for some sort of explanation for the door’s advice. Page after page seemed to have nothing but messages of job growth and record profits, especially for several of the companies he had invested in. He looked again at the door. Still the same message: GET OUT NOW.

I thought the recession was supposed to be over, George thought. Great. Well, I'll just sell my stock first thing tomorrow, let whatever it is hit, and then get plenty of bargains once the market bottoms out. George relaxed, went back to reading the paper, and took a long, leisurely time relieving himself. After he finished, he took one last, quizzical look at the message on the door.

"Well, the restroom never lies," he said, tapping on the door before walking straight into a skinny, wild-eyed man in raggedy clothing who was almost sprinting towards the bathroom. Both men crashed to the ground. The raggedy man immediately got on his hands and knees. "Where is it?!? Where is it?!?" he scoured the ground around them.

"Watch where the hell you're going," George sneered as he got up and brushed off his suit.

"What'd you say? What'd you say?" said the man, fixing two bloodshot eyes on George.

George was about to repeat what he had said when the man leapt up and grabbed him by the lapels. "You took it!" he screamed. "Gimme it back!"

"I didn't take anything!" George shouted, trying to shove the man away. "Get the hell off of me!"

"Gimme it! Gimme it!" the man screamed, shaking George. George wrestled with the man, trying to break his grip. Before he knew what was happening, George felt a sharp pain in his abdomen. And then another. And then another. And then the pains were in his chest. Only when he fell backwards through the doorway of the bathroom did he notice the knife or the bloodstains rapidly spreading across his shirt.

"You shouldna took it!" the raggedy man screamed, waiving his bloody knife as he backed away, turned, and disappeared into the shadows of Delphi Street.

George could feel his life seeping away. He knew that no ambulance could make it to him in time, even if he had been in a part of the city where ambulances came quickly.

George felt around in his pocket with fingers that were quickly going numb. Pulling out a fistful of bills that he could barely hold onto, he dropped them all into the bowl of the toilet. With every bit of strength he could muster, he lifted his arm, now so very heavy, up to the flush handle.

"What comes next?" he whispered as he let his arm drop.

Whatever answer the door had went unread by George Rafferty's now lifeless eyes.

Geschlossen

Thomas Pescatore

He's getting older
worried more about shit
shape, consistency, regularity
when was the last time
he went?

He thinks about shit more
than most things now,
besides cancer and how
many years he's got left,
and this person he knew
died at 40 young.

She asks him what he
wants out of life,
but sometimes it feels shallow,
like it's multiple choice,
with no option
for all of the above.
He's thinking about shit
tho while she talks,
and his bloated stomach
wondering if he ate too little,
or if he ate the wrong things,
or maybe it was too much,
he thinks of fibre
and caffeine.

Often he considers stepping
off the tracks, wandering away,
swerving his car into a barricade,
but is that even possible,
can it be done? Or is he just eyes
and mind watching his body
move and work and follow lines?

It's so tiring getting up,
sitting, laying back down,
if he closes his eyes
another day has gone.

He is sure he'll shit tomorrow,
at the very least, the day after that.
Just relax, don't stress out.
A coffee will fix it, some cold
water right after you wake,
maybe sprinkled with
lemon juice, lime juice,
from a home remedy
he read online.

Every tomorrow
there's the same dress shirts
hanging side by side,
sometimes they're thrown over a chair,
sleeves still rolled up to elbows;
through the window cuts the
morning workaday sun.
How often does it do that?
How many years have slipped away?

The Room Freshener Seller

Mrinal Kanti Ghosh

Among the busy crowds of Howrah railway station I move, as if in a trance; I do not know where to but I move and move, and reaching the last platform I get back my senses - I have to wait for someone; I have to look into her eyes; I have to hold her hand; I have to keep my promises; I have to board on a train; I have to go somewhere very far, maybe Mumbai, Delhi, Bangaluru - anywhere but far from this Bengal.

While coming back to the ticket counter I get to listen to an announcement that a train from platform no. 7 will depart for Chennai at 7:25. I hurry towards the ticket counter, stand in the queue, buy two tickets and start walking towards that platform. Still half an hour left. I wash my face, buy some food and a bottle of water, and board that train. Somehow I manage two seats in a general compartment. I sit by the window and beside me place my grey shoulder bag. I look outside vacantly. Many muzzy thoughts start coming to my mind making my vision blurred. I desperately try to stitch them in order, to remember them from the very beginning.

It was early 1990s. I lived with my parents in a small village called Kutubpur in Meherpur district. Many Islamic organizations started growing up in Bangladesh, due to which a pressure was apprehended on the minorities there. So my father decided to leave our country for India. Within a few miles from our village there was the Bhairab River on the opposite bank of which was a check-post of the Indian BSF. Our relatives in India made arrangements. One afternoon I was playing with Deepali under a jackfruit, when my mother called out to me. I went and Deepali followed me; whenever I went somewhere she used to follow me.

'We are going to India now,' my mother said hurriedly. 'You have soiled your whole body, wash yourself.' I said nothing. Holding a jackfruit leaf in my hand I went to the ghat to wash the soils off. Deepali followed me. I set the leaf afloat on water.

'Look, it is floating away.'

'You are leaving us, na?' I fell silent.

'You will never come back to see me.' I looked at her pale face.

'I will, promise.'

'I'll wait, and if you don't come back to take me, someday I'll go to you.'

Whenever we used to be in my room we burnt incense sticks smelling of sandalwood, or kept gardenias, jasmines, myrtles etc on windowsill and the room got filled with fragrance with the breeze coming in. That day when I was closing the window of my room for the last time she with some myrtles on her palms came and stood behind me. Without turning back I, for a long time, only inhaled the fragrance of both the myrtles and Deepali. Then she put the flowers on the windowsill and left the room.

When darkness began to approach the eastern sky we set out for a less dark sky, leaving everything behind - the books I read, the plates we ate on, the kites we ran after, the cows I fed, the house we lived in, the land we tilled, the childhood fields Deepali and I roved around - taking with us only some money and the keys of the locks left at the doors. My father took me on his shoulder while crossing the half-dried river. As we approached the other bank I looked back: Deepali was standing there, one foot on water. I tried to look into her eyes- tears dropping from, as raindrops from jackfruit leaves. Reaching the bank father got me down, but at the very first step I stumbled over a rock. From there I looked back at Deepali and saw Bangladesh was lying like a widow's twilight.

We went to Karimpur in Nadia district where we rented a room with a deck which we used as both kitchen and lounge. Within six months my father collected Ration cards and Voter Identity cards, which meant my parents were to vote for those people who gave us those things. My father started working as a mason and I went to a school. But soon I had to leave the school because my father managed to earn too little to run a family. So at the age of eleven I started working as a mason. Both my father and I earned a good reputation in masonry, and we were building so many houses in that area for the last five or six years. But all the money we laid by got drained out for the treatment of my father who had been suffering from what the doctor called some motor neuron disease. One day he died, it had been six years since we came to India. After my father's death my mother and I left Karimpur for Ranaghat for a better living. We like many others who had come from Bangladesh occupied a patch of land beside the railway station and built a hut with bamboo, jute sticks, and tin. Here also I began to work as a mason but could not stick to it. I started peddling newspapers door-to-door and hawking potato chips in local trains. For seven years I used to fetch newspapers from the railway station at dawn and served them to fixed customers; then around 9 am I went out with potato chips which my mother made and packed at home. And all these years I had been so much occupied with my livelihood here that Deepali had become a half-remembered dream of years-old-night; to me she was then like a grass put between pages of a book by a child and forgotten.

In the midst of peddling things, hawkers gathered and chatted for a while. One day, one of my fellow hawkers was telling his experience of visiting a brothel in Sonagachi. We all congratulated him: 'Sabash!' Then he began vomiting his experience there to quench the thirst of our curious eyes: 'Narrow, convoluted alleys...thousands of whores sitting on wooden benches or on cemented platforms, or leaning their backs against walls... pimps... slangs... small, smoky rooms... dim yellow light... reek of tobacco and liquor... but it is clear that sex is not a clandestine matter there.'

'Where do all those girls come from?' I asked while trying to conceal my sexual urges.

'I have heard that they are trafficked in from poor families of the villages of west Bengal, Nepal and Bangladesh.'

His last word lashed me; I got startled. Suddenly my mind began to roam about the fields of Bangladesh I had once known... I began to search for Deepali there, but could not find her... I went to the ghat - the jackfruit leaf was still floating alone... I rushed into my room - empty, except the smell of the myrtles Deepali had kept on the windowsill... I again crossed the river, looked back only to see nothing but the dark, vast pasture and the words flowing with the waters of The Bhairab: 'I'll wait, and if you don't come back to take me, someday I'll go to you.'

For the next few days my mind was occupied with the thoughts of Deepali; I was always thinking of where she is, how she is. What if she has been thrown into a dim room of some stinking maze with ten or eleven strangers visiting her with their pants unzipped everyday? What if she cries with pain in her thorax? What if she has been trained to laugh with a drunken lech? What if her breasts are scarred with dirty nails? What if she feels like vomiting because of the stench of tobacco and liquor in a smoky room? All such dark apprehensions made my days and nights restless. And these apprehensive days and nights resulted in a decision that anyhow I must get access to all the rooms of all the brothels of Sonagachi to find if she was there.

But how? So many women lived there. The pimps or the aunties would not give me her address even if they knew her. On the other hand, it was impossible for me to live a whole week without earning a rupee. Thus I got stuck in a dilemma. At last, he who had told us about his visiting Sonagachi suggested me to hawk canned room freshener in the brothels there: 'Everything is fine there but the rotten smell of the room. I think every visitor feels like me. You should crack this side of opportunity; it will give you good business, much more profitable than what you do here.' And he explained how it would help me earn money as well as look for her. The idea appeared brilliant to me. I remembered how we perfumed my room with incense sticks and flowers in Bangladesh.

Next day I went to a wholesaler who promised me to supply room freshener cans at a very cheap rate. I deposited some money and took fifty cans. When I returned home at noon with a huge shoulder bag full of room freshener cans, a new shirt and a pair of shoes, my mother asked surprisingly, 'What are you going to do with all these things?'

'I'm gonna leave hawking potato chips.'

'What? Have you gone mad or something?' she said out-loud. A long pause followed. 'What will you do after that? Since your father died, you could not stick to one job for a long time. Had he been with us, you could not do it.' She started ladling water into the cauldron while sobbing and wiping tears and anxiety from her face with the end of her sari.

'I will sell canned room freshener.'

'What is that?'

'It is used to make the air of a room smell sweet.'

'Does anybody use it?'

'Yes, especially those with a lot of money.'

'Where will you sell them?'

'I'll go door-to-door,' I lied. I knew I could not tell her the truth because I also knew how disapprovingly she would react to my truth. It was not because she did not like Deepali or she did not want her to be with me, but because she would not allow her son to go to brothels for whatever reason that might be, and because, even if I found her there, she could not accept a prostitute into her family. I stood still for a while and tried to guess what my mother would be thinking at that time. But I had to go and find her because whenever I thought of Bangladesh, she appeared before me like a dilapidated, haunted house with its roof, floors and walls all damp and darkly mossy where the fields and the ponds and the jackfruits and the bushes and the scented room of my childhood lain buried, oblivious to me, but I would not let them go into oblivion, and Deepali was the only key to explore them. She is the Bangladesh.

Next day, by 10 am I reached Sonagachi. Seeing so many prostitutes at a time nervousness and excitement flowed over me. For a few moments I got distracted; I realized desire was lurching within my body. I slipped my left hand into the bag and taking out two cans I started walking along the alley while shouting my business cry; my eyes were running on every face standing on both sides of the alley. But I did not get convinced of Deepali in the gestures their eyes were trained for.

'What is in your hand?' asked a middle-aged woman.

'It is room freshener; if you spray it, the air of your room will smell of the flower as labelled,' I tried to explain thoroughly. Some other women gathered around me with curious eyes. 'I think your rooms are small. At least seven customers visit each of you a day. Most of them smoke and drink in the room, and you both perspire while having sex. So the room got filled with bad smell, it stinks. That stench is very repulsive to a new customer. The good smell will help the customer to be in good mood being in which he may give you a generous tip.'

Hearing my explanation some giggled, some twisted their lips in disapproval.

'Those who bargain for five minutes for a job of fifteen minutes,' one of them said mischievously, 'will never give a tip; in my whole life I've never seen anybody to do so.'

'But what this fellow is saying is right. I don't care if I get tip or no tip, but at least we'll not have to suffer from foul air,' someone got my point.

Whenever I was visiting a new brothel and many women were gathering around me, I was feeling heavy, nervous pulsations within my heart, as if they were trying hard to come out breaking my ribs. I was a totally confused soul then - whether she was there, whether I would be able to find her, whether I would be happy or sorry or angry if I met her. I could not even understand whether I really did want to find her here or not, whether I wanted to see me to succeed or to fail. But one thing was clear that amid all these confusions my eyes were always looking for her among the crowd. I visited seven brothels that day, and all the cans got sold out within two hours.

Thus I became a room freshener seller. For the next few months I was doing the same job without any breaks. I was making very good in this business, with a handsome profit coming into my pocket. In these few months I visited so many rooms of those brothels, told so many girls about her, even met seven or eight girls with the same name, but did not get the Deepali I was looking for. Then one day I, squatting on my haunches on the veranda of a brothel, was showing a perfume container to a girl, when I saw a man came down from a semi-dark staircase, waved his hand to someone upstairs and left. Then and then I ran upstairs to see who that man had been waiving his hand to, and saw a middle-aged woman chewing betel while sitting on a chair. I introduced myself to her. She was the owner of this brothel.

'In our days these things were of no use; customers wanted only good behaviour,' she said negligently, twitching her lower lip. 'Nowadays tastes are changing; daintiness is proportionate to perversion.'

Then she called out some girls and went downstairs. Girls came and stood around me. While showing the cans to them I heard a girl talking in Bangladeshi accent. She was short, brown-skinned, curly-haired and wide-eyed. I became sure that she was from Bangladesh.

'Are you from Bangladesh, na?' I asked. But she remained silent for some time and went into a room without buying any cans. After the other girls left I went to her and asked the same question.

'I'm not going to tell you anything. Leave me.'

'From your accent I assume you are from Bangladesh. That's why I am asking you, nothing else,' I said smilingly, after a pause of two or three seconds.

'Why shall I tell you? Who are you?' she said in a calmed down tone.

'I am also from Bangladesh.'

'From which part?'

'Kutubpur, Meherpur district.'

I noticed waves of shock, bewilderment, sadness, happiness and hope flowed over her eyes. Her eyes were not watching me any longer, rather madly looking for someone she once used to wander with among the bushes of some distant land long left. The mischievous glint of her holy eyes was, by then, fading away.

'What is your name?' I asked with a touch of sureness.

'What is your name?' she countered, without giving me the reply.

'Bikash Biswas,' I answered, perhaps with expectations. She stepped forward, and then stepped back. A silence reigned in between us. She smiled, but her smile got halved between her hopeless breasts and expectant eyes. She banged the door. I kept standing on one end of the door surmising what was happening on the other end - perhaps a girl of about twenty, her heart pumping with tension, excitement, fear and expectation, was crossing the Bhairab in quest of her love and frequently looking back at the vast land left behind in hope of regaining it someday. The jackfruit was still shedding tears long after the rain had ceased to shower on it. The jackfruit leaf was floating aimlessly. The room behind the closed door smelled of myrtles.

Next day I again went the same brothel, and before selling any of the perfume cans I entered her room, this time as a customer; she was sitting on her bed wearing a tight, white kameez and a blue salwar. I locked the door from within. She neither moved nor looked at me.

'How did you come here, Deepali?'

'You did not come back,' she said in a low tone after a long silence, looking at my eyes.

'Do you want to go with me?' I managed to say.

'They will not let me get out of here. I earn a lot for them.'

'I'll manage that.'

Then we talked for long time, almost about everything - my life here, her life here, how she came here with a man who had promised her to take her to me, our future. We laughed together, we ran in the fields of Bangladesh; we regained the space and time lost long ago. I gifted her a room freshener can which she kept on the windowsill of her room. For the next five days we met daily, spent a lot of time together, and planned our escape.

The train blows its whistle alarming my reverie. Deepali has still not come. My heart is overflowing with apprehensions. I get down on the platform, leaving my shoulder bag on the train. I look around trough the crowds, but can't spot her. Announcements of trains, sounds of rail engines, whistles of trains, jostling, chattering crowds, my own anxieties - they altogether are making my senses giddy. Suddenly, on the less-crowded platform no. 6 I see her looking anxiously for someone. A sigh of relief. I call her out loudly while waving my hand. As soon as she sees me, a complacent smile sparks in my eyes, requiting her love, fulfilling our quests. She gets down on the railway track in between the two platforms. The train starts moving with a jerk. Standing still I watch her coming - I see a girl crossing the river with a boy, I see a girl tiptoeing with myrtles on her palms toward the windowsill; I see a green leaf floating towards the other shore of the sea with a golden couple on it.

The mock turtle is all things to all men

Adham Smart

I'll be standing at the bar
when you and your friends come in.
You see me head down
and I'm too shell to turn you away.
You want to slip me out
and feel me see me naked on the floor
without my own kind
of backbone, but my armour disc collection
doesn't bend like that. I'm different because
that was the only way to be different at the time,
I needed to be more unturtley, less seaweed
more oats and rye.

I am reptile in my taste in books, mammal in my music,
my scale hands cut bread and my skin ones open cans.
Having evolved later doesn't make you better,
it just makes you different, and if my closest relatives
still sometimes walk across each other's tracks
then they must've been equally good
enough to make the cut for this programme we're making
called the modern world. So I'm standing at the bar
and when you come in I'm going to breathe and
I'm going to think very hard, and you'll
think first and then breathe, and I'll be going home
soon after because I wasn't feeling
that kind of night.

Crush

Philippa Found

Make_up_pro says it's all about gloss. A translucent shimmer on the lips to give a milky wet sheen. Katie copies the look from Instagram: smearing her lips in plumping gloss until they are mirror glazed, then swipes a flick of iridescent liquid liner, just above, on her skin, to highlight the sharp V of her Cupid's bow. She smacks her lips together. They feel sticky. She tucks the gloss into the gap at her waistband, between her school skirt and her skin so she can touch it up later. All she's eaten in the last twenty-four hours is an apple and she's pretty sure it's already had a positive effect on her waist. She rolls her school skirt up an extra fold at the waistband to lift the hem an inch higher up her thigh, ignoring her mum when she says this makes her look like a duck from behind. Her Mum knows nothing about fashion, or life. Then she goes to the bathroom, slides her fingers between her legs and uses the moisture as perfume. She traces Xs on her wrists and her neck, drawing glossy kisses with her fingertips on her skin. She read on *cosmosextipz* that men find that scent irresistible.

Without other pupils or noise pounding the corridors, the school seems fake: just a stage set. Mr Vickers said she didn't need to arrive until five to six so she gets there at quarter to so she can hang out in his office, and prays, as she rushes down the hallway, that when she gets there he's alone.

At his door, she takes a breath and knocks.

'Come in.'

His voice is perfection – hot stars glistening on swimming pools, sunlight; it melts her. She pushes open the door and registers instantly that he *is* alone. In the first second of walking in, she takes a mental snap shot of him sitting at his computer with textbooks stacked up jaggedly either side of him, his eyes screen-lit from leaning too close to the monitor. His dark, pudding-basin hair is dishevelled with threads of grey glittering the temples; his skin looks rugged and dry, like he needs some moisturiser and a wife. She likes it though, how undone he is. It's sort of heart-breakingly intimate.

The yellow strip lighting highlights his scars. Circular dents all over his cheeks that makes her think of cigarette butts being ground into skin – she wonders if he smokes – teenage acne, presumably. The imperfection of it slays her. It makes the twenty-one year gap between them seem not so big. Not big enough to have recovered from the scars.

She wishes she could photograph him exactly as he is now and capture the moment when she walked into his office and he didn't even look up; like it was so normal her being there, and he was so comfortable with her around, that it seemed as if she'd just walked into a room in a house that they'd shared for twenty years.

When he looks up he coughs, and coughs again in an attempt to style it out. She smiles, congratulating herself on her outfit, then pretends to study the room as she stands pushing her boobs out, tilting her face to catch the best light.

The office is cramped, rammed full of bookshelves and cardboard boxes with World War Two posters on the walls. It smells of old books and sweaty fingerprints. She runs the tip of her finger along the spines of the books on the shelf, like she saw someone do in a film once, and dust floats like stars across the room, strip-lit electric. There are also two low, square, cushioned chairs pressed up against one wall; old and ugly but perfect for having sex on, probably. She wonders if Mr Vickers has thought of that too. When she sits on one, he slices a semi-circle in the air with his swivel chair to face her and their knees touch. They both look down at their knees and he slides back an inch, then looks up. His lips are chapped, a grid of white on pink. She wants to bite them.

'So, what would you like me to do for you tonight?' She leans towards him fingering her lips. She prepared the line earlier. She likes the innuendo.

The corners of his mouth turn up a fraction before he corrects himself, 'Mainly it'll just be shuttling parents to and from the department, being on hand to point them in the direction of their next appointment.'

Catching him, even just for a second, not being a teacher makes him being a teacher seem like just a role that she can crack. She can practically see the cracks, like the creases in his tarmac-grey suit.

'Sure. I can do that,' she draws out each word, to make him want to taste them.

'Right, we better get going,' he says.

She watches him gather his things from his desk and when he's ready, she stands, but doesn't leave. If she fixes where she is, he'll have to brush past her. He comes towards her but just before he reaches her he pauses. He's so close that she can smell him. It's the smell of nothing but skin. Not like the boys in her year who drench themselves in Lynx deodorant; this is a subtle scent. Warmth. Trapped in body hair. Oils.

His serpentine eyes climb upwards, meet hers. 'Ladies first,' he says and she inhales, letting invisible parts of him enter her.

He extends his arm, gesturing her through the door, the palm of his hand fitting like an echo into the space just outside the curve of her back. She wonders what he'll taste like.

Shuttling parents around is hurried so Katie can spend most of her time waiting at the front of the history classroom, either perched on the edge of the front desk or leaning against the white board, memorising him. She strains to hear what he's saying to the parents sitting in front of him; watches the kaleidoscope of his expressions transform from furrowed brow to dimpled cheeks and creased eyes.

The classroom has been rearranged so the teachers are sitting behind pupils' desks in the centre of the room and in front of each teacher there are two chairs: one for the mum, one for the dad. Whenever Katie's mum comes to Parents' Evening she must sit next to an empty chair. After so many years the teachers must predict that her dad won't show. She wonders if the teachers feel sorry for her mum always coming alone. What if they feel sorry for her, knowing her dad doesn't give enough of a fuck to show up? She looks out of the window into purple sky, no, having an absent Dad gives her an edge. One that's dark and sharp but glitters when the right light touches it, like cut glass. It says she has depth. Closes the gap.

'Alright?' Katie looks round and Darren's in front of her. He cocks his chin up.

'Oh hey,' she says, slipping off the edge of the desk.

'So you helping out?' he says.

'Evidently.'

Darren edges closer, looming into her personal space. She'd step back, but the desk's in the way.

'So what you doing later?' Darren says pushing her on her shoulder.

She looks at his hand on her shoulder then back at him. 'Going home?'

'Lame.'

He starts soft-punching her on the top of her arm and she's about to slam his hand away, but as her eyes skim the room she catches Mr Vickers watching her and Darren. Their gazes lock.

She dips her head, looks up at Darren, 'Why, what are you suggesting?' she smiles, then flicks her eyes to Mr Vickers.

It works. The way light can pass through glass without making a sound, she can feel Mr Vickers zoning in – cutting through the parents in front of him, across the classroom – onto her and Darren. Katie leans closer to Darren, so he can touch her some more. She flicks her hair as she's talking, wraps a strand round her finger, looping it, like a lasso, and she can practically hear Mr Vickers' brain stumbling as he tries to re-engage with the parents in front of him because he's completely attuned to her. Laughing is most effective.

'So,' Darren says, 'do you fancy going to the pub later?'

She has to stop, he's alright but she does not fancy him. Then over Darren's shoulder, she sees Mr Vickers looking. 'Sure,' she says and smiles.

When Darren has gone, and Mr Vickers has a break in his schedule, Katie struts toward him.

'Can I get you a coffee or tea?' She rests her fingers on the edge of his desk and leans over slightly.

'A tea would be great. Milk, two sugars.'

Her lips form a pout as she says, 'Sure.' She really wants to put her tongue in his mouth.

A trail of milky tea spatters behind her as Katie hurries along the corridor. Her fingers redden through the thin skin of the plastic cup. She pauses; takes a sip to taste what he'll taste. It burns.

When she walks back into the room his eyes are doing that thing they do when he stares into space sometimes: they've gone flat and blank, as if something's switched off behind them and he's slipped away leaving just a shell. She steps in front of them and like a doll tipped upright they reanimate, lighting up, and she sees life rush into them.

She sets the cup down in front of him, right on his papers. Then slides her hand into her skirt pocket, takes out the *Nice* biscuit that she swiped from the cafeteria and places it on his open notebook. Grains of sugar skitter across the page. Katie wipes the ones stuck to her palm against her school skirt, then leans in to whisper, 'Don't tell Mrs Mayer,' she flicks her eye to Mrs Mayer, sitting at the next table down, 'but there was only one left and I stole it for you.'

Mr Vickers raises his eyebrows, looks at Mrs Mayer, at the biscuit, then up at her. '*You* are going to get me into trouble,' he says.

She smiles; the word trouble pulses in her head, like a promise.

At nine Darren's not in Reception like he said he'd be. Katie circles and across the open space she sees Mr Vickers sitting alone in the Assembly Hall doing some marking. Adrenalin slams through her.

She does her best walk down the Assembly Hall steps, towards him. The hall is mainly oak and has a warm glow. The stage lights burn yellow in the night.

'I'm waiting for Darren,' she announces when she reaches Mr Vickers' table.

He looks up with just his eyes and she sees future Sunday mornings, his favourite lines spilling from his lips as he reads to her in bed, his eyes skimming the surface of his page and her skin; nights spent learning how he sleeps. 'I'm doing some marking,' he says. 'Do you want to sit?'

Being with him is the key change in pop songs. It is sparklers and sugar highs, and finally getting the lead role in a film about a girl and a guy.

'We're going for drinks at the Byng,' she says. She focuses on the hashtag grooves in his bottom lip. Her heartbeat spikes. 'Wanna come?'

He opens his mouth, then stops; closes his eyes, and squeezes them. When he opens them again he looks straight at her, and sighs.

It's all happening too fast, and too slow, like watching a glass of milk topple off a table. It's terrible. A terrible sigh. Full of regret, want, sympathy, but worst of all: resignation. Standing there she shrinks, becoming as small as her reflection on the gloss of his eyes and for a second she sees herself the other way round, from his point of view: fifteen and delicate, with the potential to become anything she decides to be as long as she isn't cracked or damaged. It's an awful sight because it's wrong.

'Are you coming?' Katie spins round, and there's Darren waiting at the top of the steps.

She doesn't want to go, she wants to stay and do something that will move them past this look. She stares at Mr Vickers then Darren, then Mr Vickers. *I'm your teacher* – his eyes are saying – *Nothing can happen* – and she feels crushed, like a balled up tissue. She turns and quickly walks up the stairs towards Darren.

They're cutting across the courtyard towards the school gates to leave when Katie grabs Darren's arm, 'Let's go to the lake.'

There's something inside her resisting leaving. A restlessness, but to stay; an unwillingness to accept the night is over and move on.

'The lake?' Darren frowns.

'Come on!' She tugs his arm, turns and runs. Her body slices through the slits between the concrete buildings, out towards the school woods with Darren's footsteps slamming hard behind her.

At the lake, she finds the Evian bottle full of vodka that the year eleven's store in the hole in the trunk of the Oak tree. It's full: topped up every Monday. She holds it up like a prize; downs some, then chucks Darren the bottle. Everything becomes warm and blurry as they sit on the ground drinking.

'So when are you going to give it up?' Darren says leaning in. His breath is hot and vodka laced. He smells of Lynx. 'You're nearly sixteen now, it's practically illegal to still be a virgin.'

She looks at his watch to avoid his eyes. 'Fuck, Darren!' she laughs, 'We'll miss the last bus if we don't leave now.'

Night has transformed the school making it meaningless. It's black, except for the punctuated glow of lights that stud the buildings. Their plastic casings mostly cracked and fogged. And it's empty, like a graveyard. Their footsteps sound hollow against the silence.

As they turn a corner and pass the outside of Mr Vickers' office, Katie's stomach wrenches. She pushes Darren up against the brick wall of the building.

'What are you doing?' he says but when she doesn't move, a smile creeps across his face. His eyes flash, electric.

She's weightless as he spins her round, slams her back against the wall, rams the hot oblong of his erection against her, and crushes her body beneath his weight. Losing hope of what you want feels liberating. It frees you to be reckless, Katie thinks. And there's a power in that. It makes you not you. And not being you means you can be anyone.

She reaches down, unzips Darren, and bunches her knickers to one side. She doesn't wince as he thrusts in, breaking her inside, as her back – through her school shirt – is grated against the rough surface of the brick wall. She's vodka numb. Her legs hitched round him feel disconnected to her, strange; mannequin legs. She watches Darren's bowed head as he looks down with such intense concentration it's as if he's been asked to memorise a spot on the white shoulder of her shirt. The smell of Lynx cuts her lungs, chokes her, and she's angry, like she's having to prove a point to Mr Vickers that he should have been strong enough to discover himself: that she's fine to be broken, she's so fine about it that she can even break herself.

Darren's breaths become jagged and Katie feels him jolt, pull out and a warm pool spurt jerkily onto her thigh. It shudders thickly on her skin. She scrapes down the wall; lands hard.

As Darren looks down to zip up, Katie mops her thigh with her palm. It feels sticky, like lip gloss; but it burns. Then she wipes her palm against the brick wall behind her and leaves a barely visible, personal trace drying, like spilt milk, in the cracks in the outside wall of Mr Vickers' office.

Vlogging at the National Gallery

Lane Ashfeldt

'The problem with Vik is he's trying too hard. He just needs a bit of support from someone his own age. Help him fit in.' That is the kind of crap the teachers keep coming out with. From my point of view it's awkward.

From my point of view, in fact, it would make things nice and simple if a grown-up in a position of authority would just tell me to quit hanging around with him, that my grades have collapsed and it's reaching the point where my life map is seriously compromised. All of which I know is true. Instead, the teachers say it shows leadership that I carry on being friends with Vik in spite of the attitude of the other kids, who will soon come around to him. Like crap they will. We'll all be going to university in a few months. If I can scrape up the points to get in, that is.

Vik asks if I'll be at the club on Saturday night. We haven't been to the club now for two or three Saturdays in a row because of our exams.

'All right for you,' I say. 'I still have Art and Art History.'

'Oh, well if that's all,' he says.

People who don't study art always think it's a doss subject.

It's not as if it's even a real club. Vik means his parents' place, a bar that stays open till five where we get unlimited free vodka cocktails in return for clearing glasses a few times a night.

'C'mon Josh,' he says. 'You're the only guy at school who doesn't think I'm a freak from a family of Russian gangsters.'

I don't tell him, but until I stayed over at his I did used to think his parents were Russian gangsters. Now I know that A, they're Latvian and B, they can't be gangsters because their house isn't flash enough. Gangsters have private swimming pools and homes filled with stolen paintings, everyone knows that. Even Myles Mac has a pool, and his dad's only a TV producer. But Vik would be gutted to know that I too once fell for the gangster line, so I keep my mouth shut about that.

'OK, I'll come to the club. If you will come to the art gallery with me on Sunday morning.'

'You what?'

'For history of art.'

'Looking at paintings is revision?'

'Sure,' I tell him. 'Paintings from the seventeenth century.'

And he says what the hell, it'll be fun.

But I don't know then what it's really going to be like, do I? I don't know he's never been in a gallery his whole life. Not since the ones they made him trawl round in primary school, back in Riga. Vik grew up thinking art meant blocky statues of glorious comrades fighting the good fight, and is therefore deeply suspect. To him, there is no good art or bad art, just propaganda. Oh and advertising: which is kind of the same thing but at least it tells you about fun new gadgets that you can get your parents to buy.

Sunday morning and I'm still hung over after the surreal amount of vodka we managed to sink last night. It's amazing how many eight-quid cocktails you can get through when they're free. Vik is not remotely hung over. He's unboxing some new piece of gear his folks bought him for finishing his exams. That's right, in his house they don't wait for results, just sitting your exams, or the majority of them in his case, is gift-worthy all by itself.

He fishes it out of the wrapping and it's a camera, cased in bright orange plastic. Apart from its colour it looks like any old camera with an external flash, but the sticky-out bit is not in fact a flash, it's a lens that flips back and forward, and when he tests it I see that he can film either what's behind him or in front of him. Or himself, of course. Vik spots me watching.

'New vlogging camera,' he says.

I try to look as if I know what that is.

'For my vlog. Video blog. Didn't you click that link I sent?'

My parents have changed the wifi password and won't give me the new one till after the exams. I don't tell Vik. Actually it was me who suggested it. Part of me secretly hopes that against the odds I'll get into a good uni and will not spend the next three years drinking free vodka and being amazed by Vik's chat-up techniques. Part of me would like to go to Durham and fall in with a truly dull crowd who like Scrabble, so that I can, I don't know, stay in and read a book every so often. Because all of a sudden if I tell anyone I plan on doing that, they seem to think it's a joke.

We go up the big stone steps. The gallery is one of those places with fat gold picture-frames and high ceilings with swirly bits round the chandeliers, like a stately home, and many of the paintings are of rich people, sometimes with their stately homes or their pets on show. I check the gallery map and steer Vik into the depths because the bit we need is way down the end: the seventeenth century. It was raining out but it's less crowded in here than it was on the steps outside: I guess people were worried they'd have to pay in. Vik's telling his new orange camera that entry is free unless you're a foreign tourist, in which case the doormen liberally translate the signage. He looks up, gives that insane grin of his and says, 'Records sound, too. See?' Hours and hours worth, to judge by how much he talks as we make our way to the seventeenth century.

Each gallery we walk through on the way, Vik asks me about it, then twists my words and spins them back to his vlog camera in a way that makes the artists and their subjects seem impossibly funny. He has a talent for this stuff. I start to worry that in the exam tomorrow I'll serve up his take on European Art instead of my own. How does he manage to sound so convincing? He hasn't even studied art.

When we finally get to the seventeenth century Vik goes quiet a minute. He stands with his back to one of the paintings. There's a weird sort of resemblance between him and the bloke in the painting. Not a physical one. The man in the painting has on black tights and a cloak, and a sort of doily thing round his neck. Maybe it's because they're both putting on an act?

'I'm so glad I didn't live in this particular century,' he tells his camera. 'I'd have probably spent my life polishing silver or shoeing horses for some posh guy in a frilly white collar.'

He pans around the room, comes to a halt with the lens inches from my nose, and says 'So tell me about these seventeenth century dudes, Josh. What makes them tick?' The proximity of the camera makes me stumble over my words before I've even said half a sentence. The red light goes off and he says, 'OK, scratch that – want to go again?' But I don't. Instead I listen while Vik riffs on about how all these paintings are so like each other it's difficult to tell the work of one artist from the next, and if the artists had still been alive when photography was invented, they'd have been pretty much fucked on the portraiture front. Out of a job.

Then he says it's time for him to make a move.

'C'mon, Vik. I did your club, you do the gallery. That's the deal. Just get through the seventeenth and we'll go, yeah?'

'If you're done soon you'll find me on the steps outside.'

'What's wrong?'

'I'm tired of people staring at me like I'm weird.'

This earns muffled titters from a group across from us, stood in front of this one painting. It's not clear if they arrived together or if the group just formed around the painting, which is of a guy in a black hat. Some of them have been glowering at Vik for the last little while. Now one of them comes over. You can see he's thin in his tight suit, and he speaks in a clipped accent that could be British or US East Coast.

'These guys had more talent in their little fingers than you'll ever possess. More technique too.'

Vik switches his camera back on and points it right at the guy. I try to shush him but I know it's no use.

'Why do you lot keep staring at me?'

'Just stop talking to yourself and no one will stare.'

'What's wrong with me talking? Actors and presenters do pieces-to-camera all the time, and no one thinks they're weird. Well, only in a good way. People treat them like they're gods.'

The man jerks his head at the painting and I move a little closer to read the title. REMBRANDT AT THE AGE OF 34.

'We came here specifically to see that one painting. If you don't let us look at it in peace, I'm going to ask an attendant to kick you out.'

Something in Vik flips.

'Would they throw out the BBC? Nope. So why throw me out?'

Two of the group beneath the painting snort loudly then leave the gallery, possibly in search of an attendant.

'Anyway, why do you all care so much about that one painting of the dude in the black hat?' Vik says.

'Because it's the best.'

'Is it? Or do you only think that because it's what you've been told. Is it the bullet proof glass, does that mean it's better? Haven't you noticed how alike these paintings are? For all you know, this one's a Rembrandt too. They're all works of genius, if a painting that is basically a photograph is a work of genius. They're like those airbrushed photos you see in magazines, that make you feel bad for being real.'

Vik gestures at the paintings that have no bullet proof glass. The thing is, they look better without the glass. Plus you don't have to queue up to see them, or worry if you're taking too long.

'Tell you what,' the guy in the tight suit says, 'Why don't you go to art college and learn some stuff before you start mouthing off?'

Maybe this gets to Vik. I don't know. He says nothing, just walks away all quiet leaving the man in the suit to his painting. I follow. I'm watching Vik's camera so as not to look at his face: the screen has lines across it and the video pictures are moving too fast, like people are jogging past the paintings. I realise he's doing in-camera edits as we walk.

'Whatever he says, you needn't worry about an attendant coming.'

'Yeah, why's that?'

'Haven't you noticed? There aren't any.'

Vik looks around. 'Hmm. You're actually right.' Said in such a way as to imply that my being right is a highly unusual occurrence. I'm about to ask why if I'm so rarely correct he used to copy my homework, when he says, 'Where have all the attendants got to?'

I've thought about this before, and I think I know the answer.

'Commercial galleries sell paintings. Public galleries started out private, then they got money from the government. These days they're a bit of both, and they have an innovative business model: they only show stuff that's officially good, by artists so fashionable in their own lifetimes they became instant legends. Paintings so expensive they have zero resale value. Cuts the need for security, keeps costs down.'

I pause for breath. 'You know what their strapline is?

He shakes his head.

'See priceless works of art for free.'

'So how do they stay in business?'

'They have a neat line in mugs, umbrellas and notebooks printed with the aforesaid priceless works of art, but of a much more nickable size. So the security staff guard the tat instead of the actual art.'

While I'm talking Vik throws one arm round my shoulder and with the other starts to film us. As soon as I'm on camera the small digital me on screen looks nervous and my spiel about art revenue models dries up.

'So they'd throw me out, but they're too busy selling tat?' Vik asks. 'There's a Jesus-in-the-temple thing here somewhere, but I can't quite put my finger on it. I'm too busy feeling chastised at my own minuteness in the scale of things, next to these heartbreaking works of staggering genius.'

Actually I do kind of think Vik is smart, just not in the way smartness is normally measured: the way that works for exams, university and those life maps our school careers adviser likes so much. But whatever he says, I seriously doubt he really does feel chastised. At least, not until a minute or so later, when there's this sound of footsteps behind us getting closer and closer, and we're both thinking, so much for what I said about the gallery attendants, and we look at each other like, do we need to run now?

We try walking faster but the footsteps behind us speed up too.

A quick glance behind and I stop. It's not a guard. It's this cute Japanese girl who two minutes ago was standing in front of the bullet-proof painting. Now she's following us. Why?

She barely sees me of course, it's Vik she talks to.

'I heard what you said. You talk a lot, don't you? So, people shouldn't stare. They should respect you, like an actor or artist?'

A pause.

Vik blinks.

'Sort of. Well, that would be nice.'

'Yes, but you're not a genius, are you. That's not why people stare. They stare because each time you speak to your camera you pull your hands through your hair, and your puff levels are way too high. They stare because you are one silly Brit boy with very bad hair.'

Vik looks gutted, but doesn't stop recording. In a small voice he says, 'Actually, I'm from Latvia originally.'

'Yes but you're British now.'

He laughs and bats his hair down in an effort to bring it under control. In a few seconds he's back on form.

'How's that? Am I good now?'

'Hmm. If you were famous you could have puff levels up to here' — she holds her hands a foot above her head — 'and no one would care.'

'Roll on that day.' Vik sounds happier. He's purring the way he sometimes does when he invites people to his parents' club. Maybe it even works, I'm thinking, because the Japanese girl doesn't look nearly as cross. She's laughing and giving me this look like she is both irritated by and interested in us, at the same time. Vik takes a step back and frames a two-shot of me and her, and she asks how I put up with him. A question I've asked myself often enough and it's only now the answer comes.

'Vik's my friend,' I tell her. 'The only guy in school who'd rather hang out with me than do well in their A levels.'

She nods.

We keep walking and it occurs to me we're miles away from the seventeenth century, and I still have a few paintings left to tick off my list. I consider heading back, but only fleetingly. Instead I tuck my map of the gallery in the back pocket of my jeans and keep going, past the shop and the collection boxes, past a small demo against public spending cuts where all the gallery attendants are stood in a line, and down the big stone steps and outside. All this time we're on camera, Vik walking backwards in front of us, which he patently doesn't need to do because of his new camera but maybe he just wants to for effect. He comes to a stop right up against a big pillar with ridges carved in it, and starts talking into his camera again.

'So people only give me odd looks because I'm not famous. That's why they don't want me to do this. Interesting. And how'm I supposed to get famous if I don't start somewhere? Why not start here?' Me and the Japanese girl watch him and laugh, but we're laughing with him, not at him.

Vik likes to make a show, I realise all of a sudden, because it's what he's good at, it's his thing. Maybe the man in the tight suit is wrong and Vik is some kind of genius after all, because for someone who point blank refuses to make a life map, he's doing fine. His puff levels are infinitely high and he gets away with it. And it's clear to me that right now I don't give about the art exam I've to sit tomorrow, because today is important too. We ought to do something, the three of us. We all agree on this without anyone actually saying it. Vik puts his camera away and grins, and the three of us walk across the square and under the arches into that park with the ducks and the stripy deckchairs, where just one look at the sky is enough to know it's going to stay sunny all afternoon.

First Time at the Cuddle Party

Stephen McQuiggan

If he hung around outside the church hall much longer they would think he was an alcoholic, or something even worse. He just could not muster up the courage to go in, the strength to take that first telling step. The little window above him glowed with a kindly light that seemed to soak up all his doubt, but on the other side he could hear voices, attractive voices, laughing voices.

No. It was not for him.

They sounded too confident, too happy, as if they already knew each other, their quirks and foibles, and liked each other all the same. He would only feel left out again. He turned to leave, to slink away in the hardening rain, but his path was blocked by a woman. Though he only caught a glimpse of her before he quickly lowered his eyes, he could tell she was very beautiful.

'Are you going in?' she asked and he found himself nodding. 'I'm Katherine.'

'Rick.' She smelt of strawberries. He followed her through the door and down some steps, hypnotised that such a woman would even speak to him. As his boots squeaked after her he thought that maybe this time it could be different.

'I haven't seen you here before,' she said. 'Is it your first time?' She hung her coat on a peg buckled by the weight of others. Rick put his wet woollen one on the floor; it sat hunched like a caveman's dinner.

'Yes. I thought I might...' He had no idea what he thought.

'I'm afraid you'll be asked to get up and talk a little about yourself. Nigel likes the newbies to interact.' She laughed when she saw the pale horror on his face. 'Don't worry, it's really not that bad.'

Although she had removed her coat, and was now taking off a spangly scarf, he noticed she was still wearing her gloves; long leather gloves, up to the elbow; black and shiny, the gloves of a sci-fi villain.

She ushered him into a large brightly lit hall where people were speaking animatedly to one another as they fidgeted on too small chairs. He expected them to grow silent when they saw him, surely they would know, but they didn't pay any heed to him save for the occasional smile.

'Katherine darling!' A large behemoth made his way toward them and air kissed air. 'I didn't think you were going to make it tonight. We're just about to start.'

'I wouldn't miss it,' she said. Her eyes looked ancient. Bears at the zoo had eyes like that thought Rick; the wildness hidden behind an empty window.

'Please. And you've brought a friend. Beautiful day don't run away, I've yet to taste you!'

'Yes, this is Rick.' She remembered; Rick's heart stuttered.

'Great to meet you Rick.' The large man smiled. 'I'm your Team Leader this evening. Please take a seat in the Welcome Circle. I'm simply dying to hear your story.'

He flounced off, blowing kisses and sowing smiles as he went.

'Nigel,' said Katherine, turning her eyes in. Rick laughed. Somehow, in her presence, his fear was not so strong.

But as he took a seat, his chair squawking on the polished wooden floor, he felt it return, barking ever louder and jangling his nerves. Soon it would be his turn to stand up, to reveal why he was there, and they would all laugh, especially someone as pretty as Katherine. Maybe if he told them about the 'hairy hugs' his grandfather used to give him...

No. Not this time. Not the first time.

Nigel was running through the rules in a perfunctory sing song manner that indicated everyone already knew them by heart. No inappropriate fondling, no dry humping (as if they were errant terriers), no whispering in the ear. There were rules, Nigel assured them, because adults felt safer with rules.

'We'll begin with the customary empowering,' said Nigel. 'For the benefit of any newcomers, that means asking the person next to you for a kiss. You will be rejected. This makes us stronger, and strength puts us in charge. We all need touch - Will you supply? The power is yours!'

Rick felt the hairs on the nape of his neck crackle. He needed touch alright, longed for it; wanted to grab Katherine and thaw in her arms.

Shocked at his boldness, he turned to her. 'Kiss me,' he said.

'Never,' she said.

He thought the snap of his heart was audible.

There was a solo round of applause as Nigel clapped furiously. 'Well done everybody. Now it's time to shave the ice, to strip away our social armour. I see that the lovely Katherine has brought a new lamb to the fold, but before we wrap him in our Care Share and ask him to introduce himself perhaps we should show him how it's done.'

Nigel scanned the group with the silky confidence of a predator at a watering hole. 'Jessica!' he shouted at sunken little woman who jumped at the sound of her name.

She cleared her throat and began as if by rote. 'I no longer needed, nor wanted, my partner to touch me. At least, not like that.'

She stopped to wipe her glasses, and take a deep breath that rattled her meagre frame.

'All his embraces were aimed at one thing. They were strangleholds, not affection, and devoid of any real tenderness. All he wanted to do was pin me down and steal my flower.'

Rick reddened when she called it that, her 'flower', not because he was particularly coy, but because when he looked at the bony little woman he could not imagine a welcoming bloom. The image that sprang to mind was rather one of something prickly and forbidding; a cactus pollinated by chunky flies; a wreath not a bouquet.

Without fanfare the storm broke, lashing down her face. Her mouth seemed toothless as her shoulders heaved and jerked with sad electric. The whimpers that escaped her brought to fruition the tears that had waited so patiently behind her eyes; snot dangled from her nose, as if her brain had thrown down a rope ladder, the better to flee.

'Now, Jess darling,' said Nigel, 'We've talked about suckling on the pity nipple before. Sorrow is so aesthetically vulgar.' He surveyed the group once more, ignoring Jessica as she crumbled silently. 'So far we've just been notating the skeleton. Let us look at the bigger picture instead. Let's look at Jeff.'

Jeff withered visibly as the group turned to stare.

'Jeff couldn't stop cutting himself,' said Nigel, beaming at his star pupil. 'His desires over-rode logic and reason. He became a puppet to his impulses. Cutting let out the steam, the red hot rage of impotent anger that pumped his heart faster, faster, like a stallion whipped to oblivion and charging for the grave. He felt peace afterwards, for a time, an almost post coital glow. But desire is addictive, isn't that right Jeff?'

Jeff nodded. 'I can't stop thinking about God,' he said. 'I worry about Him.'

'We all do,' Nigel assured him.

Rick fought back an urge to laugh. He was beginning to enjoy himself; he longed for Katherine to be called, was almost frantic to hear her story. But his laughter stuck in his throat like a fingernail when Nigel lifted him to his feet with one burly arm and said, 'Onload brother. We are with you.'

He felt the eyes slide onto him and his tongue shrivel in his mouth. 'I... I don't know where to start.'

'Start with your name friend.'

'Rick. Rick Singleton.'

'Well Rick, pleased to meet you. Now, what scares you most?'

He had to be honest, or else this would turn out exactly like all the other self help groups he had tried. 'The walk home.' No-one laughed. 'Alone.'

There was some supportive muttering. Though her eyes were full of painful recognition, Katherine smiled at him.

'This is so hard for me,' said Rick. 'I feel...scorched...inside.' He sat back down, kept his gaze upon the floor. He could hear Nigel's shovel hands slap together repeatedly.

'Bravo, bravo!' The Team Leader's voice reverberated through the iron legs of the chairs and shook the fire exits. 'We are all Mayflies in the great maw of eternity. Now, let's begin the Care Share!'

Nigel stripped off his Green peace t-shirt to reveal a well tanned, embarrassingly well proportioned torso. He looked almost obscenely healthy.

'Do you see this body?' he asked, as if they could possibly miss it; Jessica was doing her best though, Rick noted.

'I got this body through my love, my adoration of nature. I am blessed to have trees in my back garden, and I'm drawn to them, to kiss them, caress them, to hold them. I love their gnarled skin, the birds that live in them and sing of the beauty of their house. I've tattooed them with my name. Sometimes, I'm so overcome with joy that I lick their sap.'

He painted his t-shirt back over his bulges. 'You too can reach perfection, like me or the oak, if you choose to join with nature, not fight it. The Care Share is a tried and tested way to open up your defences, to channel the force of nature.'

As Nigel strutted between the chairs Rick began to dream that one stormy night a tree would fall on him and join him and the earth together forever.

'Three seconds!' bellowed the Team Leader. 'That's what neuro-psychologists believe constitutes the present moment. Three seconds. So, can't you just live in the moment? Can't you just give for three measly little seconds? It's all I ask. Grab a partner and begin!'

Rick looked to Katherine but Nigel was already plucking her from his side. Standing in front of him was a young girl, no more than eighteen, with the pale complexion and thinly stitched eyes of a voodoo doll.

'Would you like to bear my care?' she asked, and before he could answer he found himself wrapped in her sparse embrace.

The only thing he had felt before, on a regular basis, was depressed. But here, in the girl's arms, he felt vital and alive. The blood surged through his body at an Olympian pace. It was all he could do not to grab a handful of her hair, rip it off, run home with it and keep it forever, to rub whenever he chose.

'In a few minutes we will disengage,' said Nigel, towering over Katherine's shoulder. 'Then we will make our way to the canteen for the Feel Meal and discuss our reactions.'

He carried talking but Rick was no longer listening; the guy spoke with all the economy of a toaster manual. It was all New Age, happy clappy rubbish. But this, this was good.

He knew he held her too tightly but it didn't matter, he had licence to invade her personal space, permission to burst that bubble. He breathed deeply, transported to idyllic meadows on a wave of fabric softener. It was a sexless embrace and that excited him; he felt neutered by the close proximity of her cold skin.

At first he wasn't sure why his trousers felt so tight around his crotch; it had been so long since he'd had an erection. His tumescence could mean anything; an allergic reaction, a sign of disease. But this swelling felt good, felt even better as he moved against her, rubbing the tingling growth on her, separated by the thinnest layer of cloth.

She screamed, as if he had violated her in some way, drawing the attention of the group to the centre pole tenting his zip. Their scornful eyes razed it down.

'Looks like we have a tactile retard,' said Nigel. 'Everyone, you know the drill. Trust the disgust and let him know exactly how you feel about... perverts!'

The clamour began at once. Rick's eyes nearly buckled from the ferocity of the insults hurled at him, insults dredged up from nightmares, assaulting him in glorious stereo. He dropped into himself like a stone, drowned in the roar of his own blood and the primitive thud of his heart; he resurfaced momentarily deaf, or else the insults had ceased.

They were all staring at him. All except Katherine. Her voice had not been among theirs, and this small consolation gave him the courage to speak.

'You are all right. I accept that. I have no excuse.' He felt his face ignite. He could run now, as he had so many times before, or he could tell the awful truth. Neither option seemed palatable, but looking at the disappointment on Katherine's face he decided to shame the devil.

'It's just that...it's very hard for me to say this...' He cleared his throat. 'It's just...I've never been with a woman before. With anyone. Ever. I can't. My body's allergic or something, and I was just trying to be pro-active and so I came here and everything felt so right, I felt so right y'know? So normal. For a moment I felt normal.'

No-one was laughing.

The scorn he had been anticipating had been usurped by empathy. He felt liberated, and this sudden sense of freedom egged him on to regurgitate all the shame that he had been swallowing since he was a teenager.

'I felt so relaxed, so comfortable. I'm so sorry. It came as a shock to me too. A shock to feel like a human being. I'll go now. I realise I don't belong here, but for what it's worth I'd like to thank you all.'

As he turned to leave he felt a heavy hand on his shoulder. He looked up into Nigel's warm glistening eyes.

'I disagree with your reality,' said the Team Leader. 'Stay Rick, you're what this gathering is all about.' He smiled. 'That's a direct order from the Cuddle Colonel.'

Steering Rick with him, Nigel turned to address the group. 'I've been running these parties for several months now, but I've never had a more glowing accolade than the one our new friend has just bestowed on me. It makes me proud to know that my cuddles can make someone feel "like a human being". I ask you all to look into your hearts and forgive Rick. Ask him to stay. Ask him to control himself for the sake of group safety, but ask him to stay.'

There was a round of applause, and a hearty chorus of Please stay Rick.

Then, in his ear, 'Yes, please stay Rick.' Katherine was standing so close to him he could almost see through her pale skin. He felt the faux leather of her gloves brush against his trembling fingers.

'Can I have a hug?' she asked.

He held her gently. She felt so light, as if her bones were hollow; a nothingness that was mirrored in her vacant eyes. No, not vacant. There was something there, something hidden. Something frightened.

It was like dancing with a cat. They swayed in time to his ragged heartbeat. He had no idea that hair could smell so wonderful, feel so soft, or that he could feel so real. He held her in his arms for several lifetimes, feeling his own slip away. He would never let go, he would hold her to the end.

She pulled back from him, keeping her strange eyes fixed solely on him. This close, they looked nothing more than decorative caps for pain.

'You're the one,' she whispered. 'You're the one.'

Nigel stepped between them, his bulk obliterating the angelic vision, and Rick felt as if her barely heard words had been a cruel trick of his lonely mind.

'It's time for the Feel Meal Rick,' said Nigel. 'Sprouts and celery. When the colon's healthy, the body's wealthy. We have much to discuss, come, come.'

Before he left, clapping his hands to round up his herd, he paused and asked Rick in a low voice, 'Out of curiosity, did you ever attempt to alleviate your frustration with a little...self pleasure?'

'No, no,' Rick blushed. 'I had no feelings at all like that.'

'Good!' Nigel seemed delighted. 'Masturbation is such a pointless articulation of grief.'

With that he was gone, swinging his torso like a man who treats exercise as porn.

'I'm not hungry,' said Katherine. 'Are you? The food's all hippy rubbish anyway. If you want you could come back to mine and I could make you something. Or we could just carry on where we left off.'

Rick watched the rest of the Cuddle Club mingling toward the canteen on the far side of the hall, watched them leave as if he might gain courage from their exit.

'Sounds good,' he said.

It wasn't far. As his footfalls echoed on the empty streets he felt himself a male colossus. So this is what all those songs are about, he thought. I never knew. I never had any idea.

Her flat was a Spartan little niche catering for only the basic requirements of existence. She brought him straight to the skeletal bed that dominated whatever living she did in that small room. She told him to undress and climb in.

'I can't,' he told her. 'I wasn't joking at the meeting. I really do have a problem. What happened with that girl was just a fluke. I doubt if I could manage it again.'

It was the most honest he had ever been with anyone. Her gentle, instant smile stopped him from regretting it.

'Don't worry,' she said. 'I only want you to hold me. You can do that now, can't you? You've been doing it all night.'

She went into the bathroom and didn't come out of it again for half an hour.

Stripping off his crumpled clothes he dived under the duvet, ashamed of his thin body glowing ethereally in the dim light. Lifting the covers he briefly regarded his penis; it lay like a bluebottle larvae across his fingers. He cupped it and tried to think of something else.

From the bathroom he could hear rummaging, spraying, running water. His mind flittered in a nervous frenzy. What did men think about when they were lying in bed waiting for their women to join them?

Did they check under their arms, worry about personal hygiene? Rick always had a bad sense of smell which he considered a blessing.

He wished she would hurry up. Other people's beds frightened him; he thought of them as sacrificial altars. On the few occasions he had found himself on that stage, he had been unable to perform under the glare of expectation. After that he had given up the pretence, had refused to put himself on show as an object of ridicule to satisfy a lingering hope.

He put his hand under the cover once more, ran it over the patch of wasteland between his legs where nothing grew. The bathroom door opened and he saw Katherine silhouetted in it's frame, naked except for the long black gloves. Catlike, confident, she strolled to the bed.

'Do you want to see me stripped bare?' she asked.

'I already can.'

'No, I mean really naked.'

He nodded. Using her teeth she peeled off her gloves, teasing him with the acumen of a lap dancer. She turned her palms outward, revealing her wrists and a lattice work of scars that shone like icing on her skin.

'You told me your secrets tonight,' she said. 'These are mine.'

She climbed in beside him, a frisson of panic jolting him as her skin touched his.

'I knew as soon as you held me you were the one,' she said. 'I've been going there for the last two months. I was beginning to think I'd never find you. It's all repression you know, and all too familiar. But you're different. I sensed that straight away. With you I felt none of that. I felt contact. You don't want my body, it's no use to you. I felt you reaching for my soul.'

'Yes,' he said, breathless. She understood, really understood.

'I've taken an overdose,' she said. 'I didn't want to go by myself. I think that's why I've always failed before. I've been lonely so long, and I don't want to leave lonely. Just keep your arms around me, hold me until it's over.'

He felt her breathing grow shallow as he stared at her eyelids; a tissue of skin, a thin curtain drawn over her strange eyes. He held her for several lifetimes, feeling his own slip away with hers. He would hold her until the end.

When the sun rose its dry light stung his eyes and plucked down tears upon the cold, beautiful girl locked forever in his embrace.